Also by Adam Carlyle Breckenridge

The Right to Privacy
Congress against the Court

ERRATA:

For Warren Berger *on pp. 105, 110, and 185, read* Warren Burger

The Executive Privilege

The Executive Privilege

Presidential Control Over Information

Adam Carlyle Breckenridge

University of Nebraska Press • Lincoln

International Standard Book Number 0–8032–0835–9
Library of Congress Catalog Card Number 73–82011

Manufactured in the United States of America

To Marion

Contents

The Executive Privilege

I

Introduction

The central feature in the distribution of power for the government of the United States is the constitutional and political independence provided for the three great branches. But this independence is not absolute—rather, these distinct institutions share powers, one with another, such as the power of appointment, treaty ratification, and the enactment of statutes. The arrangement provides a balancing of interests where one branch has a voice in some of the work of another. It gives a blend of powers with "the several departments being perfectly coordinated by the terms of their common commission,"[1] and an arrangement by which "the great security against gradual concentration of the several powers in the same department, consists in giving to those who administer each department the necessary constitutional means and personal motives to resist encroachments of the others."[2]

In the course of history, these arrangements have not always been "perfectly coordinated." Conflicts among the three branches have prevailed almost from the beginning. One of these has been the resistance, sometimes total, of presidents to give the Congress information it requests. This presidential control over information is called the "ex-

1. *Federalist* no. 49.
2. *Federalist* no. 51.

ecutive privilege." When exercised, this control includes access to documents and testimony, either direct or indirect, by the president and members of the executive branch before the Congress.

Throughout this work "executive privilege" refers to the *direct* invocation of it by the president rather than "privilege" claimed by a host of subordinates. These latter may claim it and under various regulations, statutes, and orders may refuse to provide information or give testimony. In considering claims to executive privilege, the participation by the president will be noted, but generally not for denials claimed as privileged without the president's specific knowledge. In many subordinate claims the courts have determined that denial was proper, in others, the courts have directed compliance with requests in whole or in part. The central interest here, however, except in some special situations as will be noted, is more restricted and concerns those matters in which a president has participated directly in invoking the privilege or otherwise giving his support to it.[3]

This work, of necessity, will consider some aspects of the related issue of what information should be made public as distinguished from what the Congress or its committees claim should be given to the latter.

The executive position about the privilege is clearly reflected in the statement in 1971 by Justice William H. Rehnquist, at the time an assistant attorney general in the U.S. Department of Justice. He said:

> The doctrine of executive privilege, as I understand it, defines the constitutional authority of the President to withhold documents or information in his possession or in the

3. The distinctions are not always clear. In *Environmental Protection Agency* v. *Mink*, decided by the U.S. Supreme Court on January 22, 1973, one issue was whether Executive Order 10501 was adequate to support the claim that the president should personally determine exemptions from disclosure.

> possession of the executive branch from compulsory process of the legislative or judicial branch of the Government. The Constitution does not expressely confer upon the Executive any such privilege, any more than it expressly confers upon Congress the right to use compulsory process in the aid of its legislative function. Both the executive authority and the congressional authority are implicit, rather than express, in the basic charter.[4]

The debate about the executive privilege has been both spirited and continuous since Washington's time. It is reflected in numerous congressional resolutions, correspondence, debate, and proposals. Executive orders and related directives on the subject have been extensive. Similarly, it has been considered in judicial decisions. Senate and House hearings have been held about the constitutional basis for the privilege and its use. Scholars of several disciplines have developed positions pro and con. But regardless of whether there is a firm constitutional basis for the executive privilege in the Executive Article, the privilege has long been in use.[5] It is believed that the privilege is essential if there is to be any real constitutional and political independence for the executive. If a president is to be subjected to compliance with legislative requests for information, if his assistants can be forced under threat of severe penalty to testify in contravention of presidential instructions, there could be an infinite harassment of both

4. U.S. Congress, Senate, *Executive Privilege: The Withholding of Information by the Executive, Hearing before the Subcommittee on Separation of Powers of the Committee on Judiciary*, 92d Cong., 1st sess., 1971 (hereafter cited as Senate, *Hearing*, 1971).

5. Whether long use alone constitutes a valid claim may be disputed. In his concurring opinion in *Youngstown Sheet & Tube* v. *Sawyer*, 343 U.S. 579, 610, 611 (1952), Justice Felix Frankfurter said, "A systematic, unbroken, executive practice, long pursued to the knowledge of the Congress and never before questioned, engaged in by Presidents who have also sworn to uphold the Constitution, making as it were such exercise of power part of the structure of our government, may be treated as a gloss on 'executive power' vested in the President."

the president and members of the executive departments and agencies.[6] If made applicable to subordinates without exception, then it would be but a short step to compel a president to testify.[7]

Harry S. Truman met a request that he appear before the House Un-American Activities Committee after he left the presidency by refusing to obey a subpoena issued by authority of the committee's chairman. Truman wrote in response, in part, as follows:

> I have your subpoena dated November 9, 1953, directing my appearance before your committee on Friday, November 13, in Washington. The subpoena does not state the matters upon which you seek my testimony, but I assume from the press stories that you seek to examine me with respect to matters which occurred during my tenure of the Presidency of the United States.
>
> In spite of my personal willingness to cooperate with your committee, I feel constrained by my duty to the people of the United States to decline to comply with the subpoena. . . .
>
> I might commend to your reading the opinion of one of the committees of the House of Representatives in 1879.
>
> > The executive is as independent of either House of Congress as either house of Congress is independent of him, and they cannot call for the records of his actions, or the action of his officers against his consent, any more than he can call for any of the journals or records of the House or Senate.

6. In *Soucie* v. *David*, 448 F2d 1067, 1072 (1971), this note appears: "Courts have power to compel subordinate executive officials to disobey illegal Presidential commands."

7. In *U.S.* v. *Burr*, 25 Fed. Cas., 30, 34 Cir. Ct., D. Va. (1807), Chief Justice Marshall, on circuit, said that in proper circumstances a subpoena might be issued to the president of the United States. He also said that "if, in any court of the United States, it has ever been decided that a subpoena cannot issue to the president, that decision is unknown to this court."

> It must be obvious to you that if the doctrine of separation of powers and the independence of the Presidency is to have any validity at all, it must be equally applicable to a President after his term of office has expired when he is sought to be examined with respect to any acts occurring while he is President.
>
> The doctrine would be shattered, and the President, contrary to our fundamental theory of constitutional government, would become a mere arm of the Legislative Branch of the Government if he would feel during his term of office that his every act might be subject to official inquiry and possible distortion for political purposes.[8]

This stand taken by the former president reflects the position taken by many who have occupied the White House. It is an affirmation of the doctrine of the separation of powers.[9]

The exercise of the executive privilege has not meant a stalemate in government, as claimed by its critics, nor has it meant some reincarnation of royal prerogative. It is policed in a variety of ways, as will be shown. Some accommodations between the branches generally has prevailed, and where not, then there is evidence that Madison's (or Hamilton's) admonition against concentra-

8. The full text of the letter as released is in the Appendix, sec. IV.

9. During the 1971 Senate hearing, this exchange took place between Carl F. Salans of the Department of State and Senator J. William Fulbright, chairman of the Senate Committee on Foreign Relations:

> SENATOR FULBRIGHT. . . . You state that this bill is questionable on constitutional grounds. What provision of the Constitution do you think it violates?
>
> MR. SALANS. Senator Fulbright, you know the doctrine of executive privilege is not founded on any specific provision of the Constitution. It is a doctrine that derives as I have indicated, from the separation of powers; just as the congressional right of investigation and inquiring is not founded in any specific provision of the Constitution.
>
> But the whole notion of separation of powers is the foundation of the executive privilege.

tion of power "in the same department" prevails and is a recognition of the tripartite nature of the constitutional arrangement for government.

In the pages which follow, the executive privilege will be examined as to its uses to show the place of the executive in the relationships with the other branches of government and some of the consequences of the constitutional provisions for the separation of powers. Conflicts among these branches will be analyzed. The steady development of executive privilege will be outlined. The theory and practice of claimed constitutional supremacy for the Congress in its sphere will be presented, as will efforts to control and police the executive, designed to prevent unfettered executive independence regardless of circumstances, in giving information or permitting testimony.

II

Conflicts between Co-Equals

When, on August 31, 1971, President Richard M. Nixon formally invoked the executive privilege and stated he would not comply with a demand from Senator J. William Fulbright that Secretary of State William P. Rogers provide the Senate Foreign Relations Committee with the details of a five-year projection of plans for military assistance programs to certain countries, the president was following a long line of practices of former presidents of the United States.[1]

This challenge of the Foreign Relations Committee stemmed primarily from the long-standing and continual prodding by its chairman, Senator Fulbright, and renewed a constitutional struggle between the presidency and the Congress.[2] In this instance, however, the application of the executive privilege to control the release of executive branch information presented less of a challenge than has

1. This is the first use of executive privilege personally and publicly invoked by Nixon. In June, 1970, the president approved its use by the attorney general in a denial to the House Committee on Government Operations for certain investigative reports about some individuals nominated to serve on advisory boards in the Department of Health, Education, and Welfare. See Senate, *Hearing*, 1971, p. 433.

2. See commentary, *New York Times*, September 3, 1971.

been the case in may situations theretofore. The difference was that instead of forcing a confrontation over the issue, senators in opposition to the president's position rather stated that since they could not get the information they wanted, they would merely reduce any proposed appropriation for foreign military assistance.[3]

Senator Fulbright responded to the president's denial in this way:

> It is my personal view that the state of the American economy, and especially our balance-of-payments situation, makes it essential that the burden on the United States of outright gifts of military equipment and training to over 30 countries must be scrutinized most carefully this year. That scrutiny requires that the Congress have available to it the Administration projections for military assistance for the next few years—information which is not now to be forthcoming.[4]

This reaction does not indicate any serious breach between the legislative and executive branches, but rather presented the view that the Congress should sharpen its financial pencil. There was no indication that the president was flouting his control over information in an unconstitutional manner, but rather that other considerations made it important for the Congress to obtain information or it would not, perhaps, act at all. Financial exigency was the clue, not the policy question of whether military assistance should or should not be provided.

The Senator's reaction was in reality a façade thinly covering some other executive-legislative issues concerning the availability of information, but also policy considerations. Long standing were the demands by the Senate Foreign Relations Committee for documents, real or sus-

3. Threats to eliminate or reduce substantially the appropriations for foreign military assistance for other reasons were not new. Every president since these programs began has met with strong congressional opposition to funding requested.

4. *New York Times*, September 3, 1971.

pected, involving the Gulf of Tonkin incident (one about which Senator Fulbright alleged that President Lyndon B. Johnson had lied), and other aspects of the struggles in Vietnam.

Indeed, the president's use of his powers as commander-in-chief and his conduct of foreign relations generally were mainly at the center of this challenge over the executive privilege. The situation also produced a convenient forum for diverse groups in the Congress, and out of it, to oppose the president on a variety of subjects. These groups were a mixture of those opposed to the foreign aid bill in all but the most restricted circumstances, those opposed to the president's plan for unwinding the position in Vietnam, those concerned about the balance of payments, those not wanting a continuation of commitments to the North Atlantic Treaty Organization, and those insisting that the Congress, especially the Senate, had constitutional responsibilities in the conduct of foreign affairs which were being thwarted by the president.[5]

Thus, the problem of getting information claimed as essential for an appropriation reflected some unannounced reasons for apparent acquiesence to the president's exercise of executive privilege.

The real issue remained: when and under what circumstances and in what manner should the Congress have access to information the president determined it should not have? Was it the information or the nature of the request, the expected response, or merely the control over information which may be in question? Or is the issue primarily one about which there is expected to be executive-legislative bargaining?

Presidents have given a variety of reasons for controlling information or limiting access to it and the uses made

5. It was alleged that the president or his advisers were muzzling members of the executive branch who were likely the only ones having information the Congress insisted it needed to legislate effectively.

of it. Most presidents do not actively seek to alienate the Congress. An executive program of any consequence must have enabling legislation and also funding. And unless the president's national constituency can be marshaled in support, the combination of individual district and state constituencies of the Congress may overcome any presidential effort. A president is generally in difficulty even if he has a Congress with a majority of his own political party. He is likely to be in major difficulty if one or both houses have a majority of the opposite party. Presidents usually have insisted that the reasons for denying information are proper ones. But they know that when they deny or direct subordinates to refuse to give information it makes the Congress "madder than Hell."

The practice of presidents of controlling information which they possess or which is in the files of their subordinates has prevailed from the beginning of constitutional government in the United States. It is inherent in the very arrangement for that government. Whether the plan for government drawn up in 1787 was properly conceived for an enduring future has long been debated. Nonetheless, the scheme provides for the three coequal branches of government. The distribution of powers among these three branches may be uneven and we may long continue to inquire into what is meant by *legislative* power, *executive* power, and *judicial* power. Equally, we likely shall continue to weigh concerns about the *uses* of these powers and how the uses are arrived at. Similarly, we may often disagree as to what are the legitimate needs of each of the coequal powers in the exercise of these powers.

As James Madison put it in 1789:

> If there is any point in which the separation of the Legislative and Executive powers ought to be maintained with greater caution, it is that which relates to officers and offices. The powers relative to offices are partly Legislative and partly Executive. The Legislature creates the office, defines

the powers, limits its duration and annexes a compensation. *This done, the Legislative power ceases.*[6]

It remains a circumstance of our constitutional apparatus, however, that coequals, unequal though they may be, do not always agree on the positions taken by each other. Much of any disagreement does not involve information or the lack of it or even the dire need for it, but rather is intertwined in policy formulation or policy direction. Policy, per se, is not the primary concern here. The concern is the place of the president in the constitutional arrangement and his capacity to determine when and under what circumstances information, factual or otherwise, is to be made available, to whom, and for what purposes.

During the 1972 House subcommittee hearings on government operations, George Reedy, former press secretary to President Johnson, made this comment:

> We do not live under a military system by which the Chief Executive is picked by the legislative body. Our system is that we have a separate constituency for the man in the White House, a separate constituency for the men on the Hill. They may be the same people, but they vote in different ways.
>
> I would prefer a system where the Chief Executive was fully, absolutely accountable to the Congress. I think that this separation, this absoluteness has caused some very major difficulties in our whole society. . . . But, we also have to deal with what we have. Whether the Constitution does or does not recognize executive privilege, it has set the President up in a position where you cannot subpeona him and bring him before your committees, and you cannot secure papers he will not give you.[7]

6. *Annals of the Congress of the United States*, 1 (1789): 581–82. Emphasis supplied.

7. U.S. Congress, House of Representatives, *Hearings before a Subcommittee of the Committee on Government Operations*, 92d Cong., 2d sess., 1972, p. 1052.

In the pages which follow, the executive privilege will be examined as to its development, the kinds of uses to which it has been put, the reasons given for those uses, real or as announced, whether executive controls over information are an impairment of substance in a democratic society, and the circumstances in which the privilege has been both supported and refuted.

In this endeavor the doctrines about control over information may not always be categorized into neat classifications. It is generally recognized that there are two broad categories of information which have been the subject of executive control. One is known as that of executive secrecy. It reflects more of a political doctrine and is used for a variety of purposes to deny or limit access to information held by the executive branch. The other broad category involves the evidentiary rule of privilege. It is the one used early in the development of the executive privilege wherein the release of information was said to give some potential harm or injury to an individual or to the public and it was deemed far better to deny release than to give it out. Fairness and justice were claimed to be superior to any need to know. It is similar to the "compelling public interest" involving questions of individual privacy or silence.

This review of the executive privilege involves information whether classified or not. It may or may not have a label of "Top Secret" or "Secret" or other formal restrictive classification. When information withheld is also classified, then there is an overlap between the privilege and pure classification. *But the matter of secrecy alone as a formal restraint is clearly different. Confusion about this distinction is understandable, especially when the result of withholding the information may be the same.*[8]

That disputes between the legislative and executive branches prevail about information control is not surpris-

8. See *Soucie* v. *David*, op. cit., as an example.

ing. When authority is shared by distinctive elements of any organization, differences about the conduct of operations is not an unusual phenonemon. This is especially so when the president has specific authority not shared by the Congress or can effectively dominate areas of power. Obviously, the grant of authority by the Constitution in the field of foreign affairs and national defense to the executive gives a president a more dominant position than he may have in purely domestic matters. Thus, any historical excursion about presidential control over information demonstrates that in the conduct of these areas there is a basis for frequent issue.[9]

The Constitution provides that the president shall be commander-in-chief of the armed forces and that he "shall have power, by and with the advice and consent of the Senate, to make treaties." He also has *sole* authority to *nominate* representatives from the United States to other nations. The Congress alone has the power formally to declare war, and the Senate has a shared power with the president in the *appointment* of ministers and ambassadors. Furthermore, the arrangements necessary for the exchange of officials and interchange with the heads of other nations is also a part of the executive primacy in the scheme of things.

In considering the uses of power in the field of foreign relations Justice George Sutherland once made this observation:

> In this vast external realm, with its important, complicated, delicate and manifold problems, the President alone has the power to speak or listen as a representative of the nation. He *makes* treaties with the advice and consent of the Senate; but he alone negotiates. Into the field of negotiation the Senate cannot intrude; and Congress itself is powerless to invade it. . . .

9. Issues which have arisen have not been confined to the legislative and executive branches. The judicial branch has been called upon from time to time to resolve them.

> It is important to bear in mind that we are here dealing not alone with an authority in the President by an exertion of legislative power, but with such an authority plus the very delicate, plenary and exclusive power of the President as the sole organ of the Federal government in the field of international relations—a power which does not require as a basis for its excercise an act of Congress, but which, of course, like every other governmental power, must be exercised in subordination to the applicable provision of the Constitution. It is quite apparent that if, in the maintenance of our international relations, embarrassment—perhaps serious embarrassment—is to be avoided and success for our aims achieved, congressional legislation which is to be made effective through negotiation and inquiry within the international field must often accord to the President a degree of discretion and freedom from statutory restriction which would not be admissible were domestic affairs alone involved. Moreover, he, not Congress, has the better opportunity of knowing the conditions which prevail in foreign countries, and especially is this true in time of war. He has his confidential sources of information. He has his agents in the form of diplomatic, consular and other officials. Secrecy in respect of information gathered by them may be highly necessary, and the premature disclosure of it productive to harmful results. . . .[10]

In opposing the release of working papers and position options for possible military assistance in 1971, President Nixon was following the Sutherland admonition about the president's responsibility in dealing with other nations. His sources of information presumably were a mixture of executive agency papers and views and opinions of confidential sources obtained from overseas. It was the president's judgment that protection of his sources and the content of their appraisals was essential and he determined that disclosure could be harmful. The crux of the matter is who determines what is harmful if disclosed and disclosed to whom. In his statement before the Senate sub-

10. *U.S.* v. *Curtiss-Wright Export Corp.*, 299 U.S. 304, 319, 320 (1936).

committee in 1971, Senator Fulbright declared that the issue in information control was "not one of the character or honesty of the foreign policy experts surrounding the President but of their lack of accountability—and the resulting lack of Presidential accountability. . . . The barrier to participate is secrecy."[11]

Sixteen years after Justice Sutherland so clearly outlined executive primacy in *Curtiss-Wright*, the U.S. Supreme Court had occasion to review some aspects of the nature of the executive power as stated in the U.S. Constitution. In the Steel Seizure Case of 1952, the president's action in directing government control and operation of steel mills was declared by the court as an invalid exercise of executive authority. Each of the justices in the majority wrote an opinion. Mr. Justice Robert H. Jackson wrote that "Presidential powers are not fixed but fluctuate, depending upon their disjunction or connection with those of Congress." He then summarized his position in these words:

> A judge, like an executive adviser, may be surprised at the poverty of really useful and unambiguous authority applicable to concrete problems of executive power as they actually present themselves. Just what our forefathers did envision, or would have envisioned had they foreseen modern conditions, must be divined from materials almost as enigmatic as the dreams Joseph was called upon to interpret for Pharaoh. . . .
>
> When the President acts pursuant to an express or implied authorization of Congress, his authority is at its maximum, for it includes all that he possesses in his own right plus all that Congess can delegate. . . .
>
> When the President acts in absence of either a congressional grant or denial of authority, he can rely only upon his own independent powers, but there is a zone of twilight in which he and Congress may have concurrent authority, or in which its distribution is uncertain. Therefore, congres-

11. Senate, *Hearing*, 1971, p. 23.

sional inertia, indifference or quiescence may sometimes, at least as a practical matter enable, if not invite, measures on independent presidential responsibility.

When the President takes measures incompatible with the expressed or implied will of Congress, his power is at its lowest ebb, for then he can rely only upon his own constitutional powers minus any constitutional powers of Congress over the matter. . . .[12]

This overview indicates the lack of clarity about the extent of the executive power and the degree to which the executive can make decisions with or without sharing that power with another branch.

Some years earlier, in *Myers* v. *U.S.,* Chief Justice William H. Taft took occasion to comment on the difference between the legislative and executive grants of power.

The difference between the grant of legislative power under article I to Congress, which is limited to powers therein enumerated, and the more general grant of executive power to the President under article II is significant. The fact that the executive power is given in general terms strengthened by specific terms where emphasis is appropriate, and limited by direct expressions where limitation is needed . . . .[13]

In more recent times, the major issues involving the exercise of the executive privilege have primarily concerned foreign affairs and national defense and security. In these fields, as indicated earlier, there are elements of both independent and shared powers. In *New York Times*

12. *Youngstown Sheet & Tube* v. *Sawyer*, op. cit., 634, 635, 637.

13. 272 U.S. 52, 128 (1926). Apparently Taft is not recorded as having invoked the executive privilege, or if so it did not become an issue with the Congress. See the *Memorandums of the Attorney General,* U.S. Congress, Senate, Committee of the Judiciary, *The Power of the President to withhold Information from the Congress*, 85th Cong., 2d sess., 1958, p. 31 (hereafter cited as Rogers, *Memorandums*, 1958). These memorandums were presented to the committee by William P. Rogers, then with the Department of Justice.

v. *United States* in 1971, Justice Potter Stewart had this to say:

> The responsibility must be where the power is. If the Constitution gives the Executive a large degree of unshared power in the conduct of foreign affairs and the maintenance of our national defense, then under the Constitution the Executive must have the largely unshared duty to determine and preserve the degree of internal security necessary to exercise that power successfully. . . .[14]

When the U.S. Supreme Court, on March 6, 1972, agreed to consider the scope of executive control over disclosure of documents about underground nuclear tests in Alaska, another facet of the privilege began to unfold.[15] In this instance, however, the issue of privilege was centered upon the extent of control the president had over information provided him at his own request. Was it full or only partial control? If the latter, then to what extent could there be forced disclosure and by whom outside the executive branch?

This issue is significant not because it revolved around any executive claim to an inherent executive power (it did not), but because it centered upon a decision by the Congress that the president should retain information in the national interest. Executive Order 10501 was based on statutory provisions of the Freedom of Information Act, which provided for a series of exemptions to the requirements for public access to information.[16] The object of the act was to reduce restrictions on *public* access to information by governmental agencies and the act required that the conditions and circumstances for release or nondisclosure be specified. Congressional purpose in this legislation and the exemptions provided were indicated in the

14. 403 U.S. 713, 728, 729.

15. *Mink* v. *Environmental Protection Agency*, 464 F 2d 742 (1972).

16. Executive Order 10501 was superseded on June 1, 1972, by Order 11652.

statement by Representative John E. Moss of California, made during the House hearings in 1965:

> We do not challenge that right to withhold for the national interest, because we specifically require it by Executive order to be kept secret in the national interest of the national defense or foreign policy. Now, that is very broad. That means that any of these documents that are of sufficient significance to the security of this Nation or to the interests of this Nation as it deals with other nations can, by appropriate designation, be excluded from the provisions of this Act.
>
> We recognize that there are going to be certain needs to keep some of this information locked up.[17]

Exemptions authorized to the executive branch in the act are as follows:

> (1) specifically required by Executive order to be kept secret in the interest of the national defense or foreign policy;
> (2) related solely to the internal personnel rules and practices of an agency;
> (3) specifically exempted from disclosure by statute;
> (4) trade secrets and commercial or financial information obtained from a person and privileged or confidential;
> (5) inter-agency or intra-agency memorandums or letters which would not be available by law to a party other than an agency in litigation with the agency;
> (6) personnel and medical files and similar files the disclosure of which would constitute a clearly unwarranted invasion of personal privacy;
> (7) investigatory files compiled for law enforcement purposes except to the extent available by law to a party other than an agency;
> (8) contained in or related to examination, operating, or condition reports prepared by, on behalf of, or for the use of an agency responsible for the regulation or supervision of financial institutions; or

17. U.S. Congress, House of Representatives, *Hearings before a Subcommittee of the Committee on Government Operations*, 89th Cong., 1st sess., 1965, pp. 14–15.

(9) geological and geophysical information and data, including maps, concerning wells.[18]

These exemptions include areas which have been of concern to many presidents and about which they have invoked executive privilege to prevent disclosure. The exemptions cited do not provide total immunity from disclosure. The act provides that the exemptions do not give "authority to withhold information from Congress." As Representative Moss put it:

> I would like to clarify one thing. This is not intended to affect the rights of the Congress. This is dealing with a public right, this proposed legislation. . . . Only with a public right. And Congress can, as an equal branch, use its own rights and privileges in seeking to get its information. This proposed bill does not affect the rights of the Congress.[19]

In *Environmental Protection Agency* v. *Mink*, the question raised was whether the president could determine whether certain information could be withheld and determine it without any review by either the legislative or judicial branches. The issue arose when word leaked out that some reports made to the president about the underground nuclear tests recommended against their being undertaken.[20] This case involved primarily a method of policing the executive privilege, albeit through statutory provisions, and will be considered in detail later. It is one, however, in which both the judicial and legislative branches were involved.

Efforts were made, unsuccessfully, in the Congress to deny funds needed to conduct the underground tests. Following this, thirty-three members of the Congress joined as individuals to institute action in the district court for the District of Columbia under the provisions of the Free-

18. *U.S. Code*, sec. 552 (b) and (c).

19. House, *Hearings . . . on Government Operations*, 1965, p. 23.

20. Justice White's opinion states that the president had received "conflicting recommendations on the advisability of the underground nuclear test."

dom of Information Act to compel the release of the documents prepared for the president about the tests. The president had, on June 27, 1969, asked for agency review of the test program to allow him time to give full consideration before the scheduled event. The reports were submitted and the president authorized the tests. It was alleged that some of the documents prepared for him stated that the tests would cause damage to the environment, including the ocean floor, or would cause disastrous tidal waves as far distant as Hawaii. The tests were conducted as planned with no apparent adverse consequences.

The district court, without *in camera* inspection, held that the documents were exempted from compelled disclosure, but the court of appeals reversed and remanded the case to the district court for *in camera* inspection and to determine whether disclosure should be ordered of some of the materials. Factual information was to be made available unless inextricably intertwined with policymaking processes.[21]

Acting for the president, the Department of Justice objected, and on writ of certiorari the decision was appealed to the U.S. Supreme Court and a decision announced on January 22, 1973.

The objection by the president was that if the documents were examined *in camera* by a judge, then disclosure resulted. Even if the judge retained to himself absolutely those portions not ordered disclosed, the question remained whether judges could or should enter such controversies. The U.S. Supreme Court had examined this question earlier. In *Chicago & Southern Air Lines* v. *Waterman Steamship Corp.*, the court stated:

> The President, both as Commander-in-Chief and as the Nation's organ for foreign affairs, has available intelligence services whose reports are not and ought not to be published to the world. It would be intolerable that courts, without

21. *Mink* v. *Environmental Protection Agency*, op. cit.

> the relevant information, should review and perhaps nullify actions of the Executive taken on information properly held secret. Nor can courts sit *in camera* in order to be taken into executive confidences. But even if courts could require full disclosure, the very nature of executive decisions as to foreign policy is political, not judicial. . . . They are decisions of a kind for which the *Judiciary has neither aptitude, facilities, nor responsibility* and which has long been held to belong in the domain of political power and not subject to judicial intrusion or inquiry.[22]

To allow or require a court to review documents even *in camera* does not resolve the issue of disclosure to the Congress. As Senator Fulbright put it during the 1971 hearings, "it would be grotesque indeed if security grounds could be invoked to deny Congress information which was available both to executive and judicial officials."[23]

The U.S. Constitution makes no specific provision for the secrecy of deliberations for either the executive or the judicial branch. It does, of course, make provision for the legislative branch. Each house of the Congress is specifically authorized to keep from the public view "such parts [of its proceedings] as may in their judgment require secrecy." During 1972 40 percent of the meetings of the committees of the Congress were conducted secretly. This was an increase over the 36 percent reported for 1971 and the fourth highest number not held publicly since 1953. Forty-one percent of the meetings of the Senate Committee on Foreign Relations were held behind closed doors in 1972 and 72 percent of the meetings of the Senate Committee on Armed Services were not open.

In the House, 49 percent of the meetings of the Committee on Armed Services were closed, but only 21 percent of the meetings of the Committee on Foreign Affairs. The Senate Committee on Appropriations held 30 percent of

22. 333 U.S. 103, 111 (1948). Emphasis supplied.
23. Senate, *Hearing*, 1971, p. 28.

its meetings in secret, but the House committee had 92 percent of its meetings in secret.[24]

These statistical counts do not indicate how many hearings were closed because of confidential matters, or considerations about national security or information which might reflect prejudicially on individuals if held in public. But the data show the extent to which the Congress finds it desirable or essential to maintain secrecy, at least in so far as it can through the device of holding closed meetings.

Early in 1973 some efforts were made to curtail the extent to which congressional committees could meet in secret. The Senate voted to retain its policies on closed meetings, but the House, on March 7, voted overwhelmingly to restrict secret committee sessions. During the debate the resolution was referred to as a "Sunshine Resolution."[25] But how much outside light would actually enter was subject to probable numerous restrictions. Closed sessions would continue if specifically authorized by a vote of each subcommittee or committee for any given meeting. In this way the burden was shifted to those members supporting closed session.

Information control is thus exercised by the three branches of government and for a variety of, and often diverse, reasons. Each considers its duties and obligations and interprets for itself when it should work within its own confines. The relationships, especially between the executive and the Congress, are the product of significant historical associations, known to both, and they weigh heavily upon the course of the development of the doctrine of executive privilege.

24. Information as reported by *Congressional Quarterly Weekly Report*, 1972, p. 2974 (hereafter cited as *CQ*).

25. *Congressional Record*, 93d Cong., 1st sess., pp. S4015, 4016, 4028, and H1448.

III

Development of the Executive Privilege

Although there are English and American colonial precedents concerning the withholding of information by an executive from a legislative body, some successful, and some not, the development of the executive privilege in the United States is one which began with George Washington's decision to insist upon a coequal status of the executive with the other branches of the government. His successors to the presidency have continued support for that position and thereby established a long line of precedents. Had Washington's decisions been otherwise, the development of the presidency in the United States could have been far different. It might have meant that the president would be subservient to the Congress or its committees, subject to partisan, political whim, possibly even frequent impeachment efforts. Instead of a president somewhat free from congressional dictation, the president of the United States could have become some kind of prime minister acting largely at the bidding of the leaders of the Congress.

But this has not been the development of the presidency nor the doctrine and practice of the separation of powers. By some counts this assertion of the power of the executive to control executive information and to refuse, if he desires, to submit to legislative demands for information, may illustrate one of the major strengths of the presidency. The executive power resides in *the* president and is not subordinate to the legislative power vested in the Congress.

The acclaimed power of the executive to control information in its possession is not specifically provided for in the Constitution. The Executive Article states only that "the Executive Power shall be vested in a President." The records of the Constitutional Convention of 1787 do not shed much light on the extent of the "Executive Power." James Madison recorded his view that "as certain powers were in their nature Executive," they "must be given to that department."[1] He also subscribed to a view that the authority of the executive should be fixed "to the extent" of that authority. But this was not done by the delegates, nor has it been done since. Those who believe that the separation of powers among the three branches should not include the executive's control over information in its possession rest their claim, in part, on the enumeration of some powers in the Executive Article and allege that this enumeration thereby limits the realm of independent authority to the specific reference to the president as the commander-in-chief, the power to obtain opinions from subordinates, the power to grant reprieves and pardons, the power over treaty negotiations, the nomination of persons to certain offices, the power to recommend matters to the Congress, and his participation in legislation through the veto.

It is this view of the executive privilege which supports the position that the privilege is based only on custom and usage and not on any constitutional provision. Senator Fulbright is quoted as saying that the executive privilege as

1. *Documents Illustrative of the Formation of the Union of American States* (Washington, D.C.: U.S. Government Printing Office, 1927), p. 133.

maintained by many presidents "is a repudiation of the very concept of government of checks and balances," and not a matter of law.[2] Equally, however, it can be maintained that if the senator is correct, then the government is one with "checks," indeed, but the "balances" would appear to be somewhat void of meaning.

One writer, vigorous in his denial that there is a constitutional basis for the executive privilege, has said that "it is idle to dwell interminably on the separation of powers."[3] He may one day be found correct (or not), but until more successful inroads are made into the practice of the executive privilege, it remains a part of the political arena and also a constitutional question which has not been fully resolved.[4] Short of a clear-cut decision by the U.S. Supreme Court or an unlikely constitutional amendment, the issue of the executive privilege *is* about the separation of powers.[5]

By and large, Americans tend to support custom. They

2. *CQ*, 1971, p. 1787.

3. Raoul Berger, "Executive Privilege v. Congressional Inquiry," *UCLA Law Review* 12, no. 4 (May 1965): 1044–120, and no. 5 (August 1965): 1288–1364. Berger's position is that there is no valid basis for any claim to an executive privilege, that it is a myth, and a president can properly withhold information *only* when authorized by the Congress. In his testimony during the 1971 hearing, he made this statement: "The first thing I want to be sure of, is to remove any implication of disclaimer of power to call on the President. I think you have that power. Be sure you don't let it go down the drain" (Senate, *Hearing*, 1971, p. 288). In contrast is Justice White's observation in *Environmental Protection Agency* v. *Mink*, op. cit., that the congressional power may be subject to limitations by the "Executive privilege."

4. See Joseph W. Bishop, "The Executive's Right of Privacy: An Unresolved Constitutional Question," *Yale Law Review* 66, no. 4 (February 1957): 477–91.

5. In *Soucie* v. *David*, op. cit., the circuit court of appeals in considering the demand for disclosure of a document about the ill effects of the supersonic transport made this observation in a footnote: "The doctrine of executive privilege is to some degree inherent in the constitutional requirement of separation of powers" (at 1071).

part with it most reluctantly. They view it as strength, a part of the vigor of the stability it gives society. They have come to know that respect for and support of custom gives advance knowledge of what to expect in a given situation. So it is with governmental functions and practices. Much of "law" has its roots firmly in custom. Much public policy reflects custom. The courts generally try to adhere to custom and precedent and reluctantly part from it. This is the substance of the development of the executive privilege.

On March 13, 1957, Senator Thomas C. Hennings, Jr., of Missouri, then chairman of the Subcommittee on Constitutional Rights of the Senate Committee on the Judiciary, wrote the attorney general of the United States, in part, as follows:

> Dear Mr. Attorney General:
>
> During the past year, the Senate Judiciary Subcommittee on Constitutional Rights has been making a study of complaints it has received from many quarters concerning a growing tendency in this country toward secrecy in Government and the improper withholding of information by various public officials. . . .
>
> In the course of this study, we have come across a number of instances in which executive departments or agencies have refused to give information requested by a committee or subcommittee of Congress. Some of the departments and agencies involved have cited as their authority for refusing to supply such information the letter written by the President to the Secretary of Defense on May 17, 1954, directing that Secretary to instruct the employees of his Department not to testify or produce documents concerning certain matters in their appearances at the Army-McCarthy hearings. . . . So that this subcommittee may have a more complete understanding of the basis and scope of the right claimed by the executive departments and agencies to withhold information from Congress, the following questions are submitted to you as the chief legal officer of our Government.

(1) By what authority and under what circumstances may the President withhold requested information from Congress?

(2) What limitations are there, if any, on the President's power to withhold information from Congress?

(3) Under what circumstances may the President delegate to others his power to withhold information from Congress? (In other words, to what extent is any such power "personal" to the President alone?)

(4) In view of the fact that the President's letter of May 17, 1954, is limited by its very terms to Defense Department employees appearing at the Army-McCarthy hearings, may it properly be cited now by executive departments or agencies for withholding information from Congress?[6]

This letter resulted in an extensive reply dated April 10, 1957, by Deputy Attorney General William P. Rogers (later attorney general and still later the secretary of state in the Nixon administrations). In his letter of transmittal, Rogers wrote, in part, as follows:

> . . . The study discusses the matter in a comprehensive manner and supplies the answers to the first three questions posed by your letter. The fourth question is answered by the President's letter. . . . This letter is merely a restatement of principles which have been in effect since President Washington's administration; and, of course, these principles continue to be binding on all departments and agencies in the executive branch.[7]

Question number (3) in Hennings's letter asks "under what circumstances may the President delegate to others

6. Rogers, *Memorandums*, 1958. This chapter draws on these *Memorandums* especially for the sources cited therein. But one of the earliest comprehensive reviews of the executive privilege was Herman Wolkinson's series of three articles in the *Federal Bar Journal* 10 (April, July, October 1949): 103, 223, 319. There is striking similarity between the *Memorandums* and Wolkinson's series for the period covered in the latter, but, curiously, no credit is given in the *Memorandums*. Wolkinson was a member of the staff of the Department of Justice at the time he prepared the articles.

7. Rogers, *Memorandums*, 1958, p. vii.

his power to withhold information from Congress?" This reference to *his* power is one of several by members of the Congress showing some recognition of the executive privilege as an inherent power of the president. Similar recognition was given to the privilege in 1971 through proposals to control it by statute.[8]

President Dwight D. Eisenhower's letter referred to by Senator Hennings states the following, in part:

> It has long been recognized that to assist the Congress in achieving its legislative purposes every executive department or agency must, upon the request of a congressional committee, expeditiously furnish information relating to any matter within the jurisdiction of the committee, with certain historical exceptions. . . . It is essential to the successful working of our system that the persons entrusted with power in any one of the three great branches of Government shall not encroach upon the authority confided to the others. The ultimate responsibility for the conduct of the executive branch rests with the President. . . . Throughout our history the President has withheld information whenever he found that what was sought was confidential or its disclosure would be incompatible with the public interest or jeopardize the safety of the Nation.[9]

In this manner the discourse by the Congress on the doctrine of the separation of powers and the executive privilege was renewed. The president affirmed that information requested would be provided to the Congress "in achieving its legislative purposes," but providing what was sought was not confidential, or its disclosure would not be incompatible with the "public interest," or its release would not jeopardize "the safety of the Nation." These have been the main tenets of the executive privilege.

Presumably all the power a democratic society should

8. On March 5, 1971, Senator Fulbright introduced S. 1125, designed to control the use of the executive privilege. See the Appendix, sec. VI, for the text of his bill.

9. Rogers, *Memorandums*, 1958, p. 73.

bestow upon its government would be provided in its constitution and be in the reservoir of authority among its components. In partitioning the authority into the three branches, all the power granted is distributed, otherwise there would be a no man's land here and there and proper functioning would be impaired. Presumably, also, this was done under the Constitution of the United States. The arrangement also provided that the three branches were so "combined as to render the one independent of the other."[10]

Alexander Hamilton wrote that

> the representatives of the people, in a popular assembly, seem sometimes to fancy that they are the people themselves, and betray strong symptoms of impatience and disgust at the least sign of opposition from any quarter; as if the exercise of its rights, by either the executive or judiciary, were a branch of their privilege and an outrage to their dignity. They often appear disposed to exert an imperious control over the other departments; and as they commonly have the people on their side, they always act with such momentum as to make it very difficult for the other members of the government to maintain the balance of the Constitution.[11]

And Madison wrote that "the legislative department is everywhere extending the sphere of its activity, and drawing all power into its impetuous vortex."[12]

Not long after these positions were presented in support of the adoption of the Constitution, the beginnings of the executive privilege and the independent status of each branch came with Washington's decision that some information available to him or his subordinates should not be given up even by formal resolution of the Congress. On March 27, 1792, the House of Representatives

10. *Federalist* no. 71.

11. Ibid.

12. *Federalist* no. 48.

approved a resolution which authorized the appointment of a committee to inquire into an expedition by Major General Arthur St. Clair conducted under the authority of the secretary of war. The committee was given authority to "call for such persons, papers, and records" as it considered necessary in its inquiry.[13]

The committee asked the secretary for some documents and he alerted the president, who called a meeting of his cabinet, Henry Knox, Alexander Hamilton, Thomas Jefferson, and Edmund Randolph. The president must have viewed this request with some concern. Jefferson recorded it as follows:

> The President had called us to consult, merely because it was the first example, and he wished that so far as it should become a precedent, it should be rightly conducted. He neither acknowledged nor denied, nor even doubted the propriety of what the House was doing, for he had not thought upon it, nor was acquainted with subjects of this kind: he could readily conceive there might be papers of so secret a nature, *as that they ought not to be given up*.[14]

Jefferson further records the decision reached by Washington and the Cabinet and the basis for it.

> No decision was made at the initial meeting of the members of the Cabinet with Washington, but at the second meeting on April 2, they were of "one mind" . . . "that the House was an inquest, and therefore might institute inquiries . . . that they might call for papers generally . . . that the Executive ought to communicate such papers as the public good would permit, and ought to refuse those, the disclosure of which would injure the public: consequently were to exercise a discretion . . . that neither the committee nor House had

13. For a detailed analysis, see Telford Taylor, *Grand Inquest* (New York: Simon and Schuster, 1955), pp. 17 ff.

14. Paul L. Ford, *The Writings of Thomas Jefferson* (New York: Putnams Sons, 1892–99), 1: 189–90. Emphasis supplied.

> a right to call on the Head of a Department, who and whose papers were under the President alone. . . .[15]

Documents concerning the St. Clair expedition were made available, however, since Washington hoped the release of the information would lay before the House, and the public, data which would vindicate St. Clair. This did not result. Efforts were made, later, by House members to persuade Knox and Hamilton to appear and respond to questions, *but the House did not accept this as a desirable course of action since it might have started a practice toward the establishment of some type of cabinet government.*

This beginning of the executive privilege indicates two facets of it. First, the president could refuse documents because of their secret nature, a category insisted upon by subsequent presidents ever since. Second, the "Heads of Departments" were not to testify before the full House but only before a committee. Department heads were to have the protection of the privilege to an extent, and curiously, not because of a restraint by the president, but by action of the House itself.

Jefferson used the word "inquest" in describing the proposed inquiry. And he acknowledged that the Congress could make inquiries. In more recent times "inquiry" has taken on the flavor of "investigation" and some of them have been challenged successfully as being beyond the legislative prerogative.

Whether the power asserted by the president or the House decision was then recognized as a constitutional issue of any consequence is not known, but one was raised and one which has continued ever since.

No full exploration or inventory of all reported instances of the use of the executive privilege by presidents appears essential. It is probable that most of these uses have been reported and are reflected in several published sources. The selections presented here are intended to

15. Ibid.

demonstrate the nature and categories of subjects which have been at issue in the invoking of executive privilege and the basis for the positions taken.[16]

The matters arising in the St. Clair incident involved a domestic situation. But soon thereafter Washington again faced a House resolution asking for information about his instructions to his minister to Great Britain and correspondence about a proposed treaty. The resolution raised the question of the extent to which the Congress, especially the House, could properly and constitutionally involve itself in the treaty-making powers. The House claimed jurisdiction because of its powers over appropriations and on the ground that it needed the requested information in order to fulfill its responsibilities in treaty implementation. The issue raised by resolution as the president viewed it was whether either house of the Congress had authority to question his exercise of power in *negotiations* with other nations. His reply to the request for information was, in part, as follows:

> I trust that no part of my conduct has ever indicated a disposition to withhold any information which the Constitution has enjoined upon the President as a duty to give, or which could be required of him by either House of Congress as a right; and with truth I affirm that it has been, as it will continue to be while I have the honor to preside in the Government, my constant endeavor to harmonize with the other branches thereof so far as the trust delegated to me by the People of the United States and my sense of obligation it imposes to "preserve, protect, and defend the Constitution" will permit.[17]

Washington's thrust was to remind the House that the

16. See, for example, the Library of Congress report on instances of withholding and witnesses refusing to testify during the Kennedy administration. *Congressional Record*, 92d Cong., 2d sess., pp. H5820–21.

17. James D. Richardson, *A Compilation of the Messages and Papers of the Presidents* (Washington, D.C. : U.S. Government Printing Office, 1900), 1 : 194.

Constitution assigned authority over the substance of negotiations to the executive, not the Congress, certainly not the House. Hamilton, whose influence was undoubtedly involved in this reaction, had written earlier in *Federalist* no. 75 why the House was not included in the treaty-making arrangements.

> The fluctuating, and taking its future increase into the account, the multitudinous composition of that body, forbid us to expect in it those qualities which are essential to the proper execution of such a trust. Accurate and comprehensive knowledge of foreign politics; a steady and systematic adherence to the same views; a nice and uniform sensibility to national character; decision, *secrecy*, and despatch, are incompatible with the genius of a body so variable and so numerous.

In his message, Washington indicated that secrecy was required in negotiations. He and his associates *needed* to observe secrecy at times regardless of whether they might *want* to maintain that confidence. Whether secrecy produces the best diplomacy is debatable, but in the thicket of international affairs nations observe generally the international rules and customs which prevail and not the rules and customs which might be desired by one of them. In Washington's time and since, the United States has been in the arena where the rules are likely already made or must be made in concert with others. One of them ordinarily observed in negotiations is secrecy. And Washington observed that the separation of powers and a constitutional grant of power gave him, the president, full authority to negotiate. In *approving* a treaty, however, he was to share responsibility only with the Senate. He concluded his message to the House:

> As, therefore, it is perfectly clear to my understanding that the House of Representatives is not necessary to the validity of a treaty; . . . and as it is essential to the due administration of the Government that the boundaries fixed

> by the Constitution between the different departments should be preserved, a just regard to the Constitution and to the duty of my office, under all the circumstances of this case, forbids a compliance with your request.[18]

Not long afterward in his Farewell Address, Washington showed continuing concern about the doctrine of the separation of powers. He wrote at the time:

> It is important, likewise, that the habits of thinking in a free country should inspire caution in those intrusted with its administration to confine themselves within their respective spheres, avoiding in the exercise of the powers of one department to encroach upon another. The spirit of encroachment tends to consolidate the powers of all the departments in one, and thus to create, whatever the form of government, a real despotism. . . . The necessity of reciprocal checks in the exercise of political power, by dividing and distributing it into different depositories, and constituting each the guardian of the public weal against invasions by the others, has been evinced by experiments ancient and modern, some of them in our country and under our own eyes. To preserve them must be as necessary as to institute them.[19]

The issue raised in 1796 over treaty negotiations and the separation of powers and the conduct of public affairs within "respective spheres" has continued ever since. To what extent did the House need more information than it had in order to fulfill its responsibility in the shared power over appropriations? Did the House have a duty to acquiesce to the president and the Senate since a treaty duly approved "shall be the supreme law of the land"? In *Missouri* v. *Holland*, the Supreme Court said: "Acts of Congress are the supreme law of the land only when made in pursuance of the Constitution, while treaties are declared to be so when made under the authority of the

18. Ibid., p. 196.
19. Ibid., pp. 219, 220.

United States. . . . We do not mean to imply that there are no qualifications to the treaty-making power; *but they must be asertained in a different way.*"[20]

The position taken by Senator Fulbright in 1971 affirms the congressional view given in Washington's time, a belief that the "Congress has neither the information it requires in order to discharge its constitutional responsibilities nor the opportunity to question and consult with the ranking figures in the new superbureau of foreign affairs."[21]

Thomas Jefferson, who did not approve of the secrecy which prevailed in the writing of the Constitution, must have found it difficult to employ secrecy when, during his presidency, he denied a request, in part, for information about the Burr conspiracy. He had raised the matter of Burr in a message to the Congress, and in pursuing the subject, the House passed a resolution asking that the president provide any information "in possession of the Executive, except such as he may deem the public welfare to require not to be disclosed." This formal recognition of executive control over information may be the first of its kind having congressional approval.[22] The resolution specifically stated that the president could withhold some information and did not tell him that certain papers and documents could or could not be excluded. The terms were what *he* deemed necessary in the *public welfare* should not be disclosed. In more recent times information disclosure has centered on what was in the "public interest" or "national security." Jefferson supported his denial for release of some information for the protection of the inno-

20. 252 U.S. 416, 433 (1920). Emphasis supplied.

21. Senate, *Hearing*, 1971, p. 23. Whether needed information is or is not made available by the executive branch on this or any other legislative matter, the Congress has demonstrated that it is capable of finding ways to exercise substantial control over dissemination of information held by the executive branch.

22. The text of the resolution appears in the Appendix, sec. I.

cent or because it might possibly compromise those who might later be involved in some judicial action. One writer commenting on this position reacted this way: "This is morally admirable but it may well be doubted that it is a necessary attribute of executive power."[23] A response to this recent view might be that concern over the welfare of individuals is properly within the purview of a president. Should he or any other official engage in behavior which would prejudice unfairly one not yet formally accused of wrongdoing? The answer should be the one given by Jefferson. He told the House this about the information he had on the subject:

> It is chiefly in the form of letters, often containing such a mixture of rumors, conjectures, and suspicions as renders it difficult to sift out the real facts and unadvisable to hazard more than general outlines, strengthened by concurrent information or the particular credibility of the relator. In this state of the evidence, delivered sometimes, too, under the restriction of private confidence, neither safety nor justice will permit the exposing names, except that of the principal actor, whose guilt is placed beyond question.[24]

To employ a term used much later, Jefferson found the items of information in the papers "inextricably intertwined" so as to render them inseparable. Jefferson expressed concern about conjecture which might harm individuals unfairly rather than any reaction about policy direction. In the nuclear test case, the issue did involve the making or implementation of policy. But both were expressing the view that documents and the information they contained were asked for and received in confidence. It should be assumed that a president should seek and receive opinions and advice in confidence and that this confidence will be respected.[25]

23. Berger, "Executive Privilege," p. 1094.

24. Richardson, *Messages and Papers of the Presidents*, 1:412.

25. President Nixon has used the word "privacy" to support the claim of executive privilege.

Both Washington and Jefferson appear not to have believed in an unrestricted power to withhold information. But presumably they were aware of Madison's view about it given in 1796. He is recorded as feeling this way about information control:

> He thought it clear that the House must have a right, in all cases, to ask for information which might assist their deliberations on subjects submitted to them by the Constitution; being responsible, nevertheless, for the propriety of the measure. . . . *He was as ready to admit that the Executive had a right, under due responsibility, also, to withhold information, when of a nature that did not permit a disclosure at the time. . . .*
>
> If the Executive conceived that, in relation to his own department, papers could not be safely communicated, he might, on that ground, refuse them, *because he was the competent though a responsible judge within his own department.*[26]

Perhaps the first unequivocal position of an exclusive privilege over information was that taken by Andrew Jackson in 1835.[27] But earlier, in 1833, he had refused to furnish the Senate a copy of a paper which was said to have been read by him to the heads of the executive departments.[28] He apparently dismissed the request as a violation of an executive right to privacy. When he sent his famous message to the Senate on February 10, 1835, in response to a resolution asking him for copies of charges made against a one-time holder of the post of surveyor general who had been removed from that office, Jackson based his refusal to comply on the admonition given in the Federalist papers about the separation of powers. Jackson referred to other congressional requests, saying: "Their continued repetition imposed on me, as the representative and trustee of the American people, the painful but

26. *Annals of the Congress of the United States*, 5 (1796): 774. Emphasis supplied.

27. See J. R. Wiggins, "Government Operations and the Public's Right to Know," *Federal Bar Journal* 19, no. 1 (January 1959): 62–86.

28. Richardson, *Messages and Papers of the Presidents*, 3:36.

imperious duty of resisting to the utmost any further encroachment on the rights of the Executive."[29]

The Senate resolution had been passed in *executive* session. Would the information requested, if provided, also be used in secrecy to deny an accused of a publicly conducted inquiry and possibly deprive him of his basic rights? Jackson, like Jefferson, apparently concluded that this could happen and he wouldn't be a party to it. Could such a request, if repeated, presume also upon the motives of the president? If so, Jackson would have none of it.

> Such a result, if acquiesced in, would ultimately subject the independent constitutional action of the Executive in a matter of great national concernment to the domination and control of the Senate. . . .
>
> I therefore decline a compliance with so much of the resolution of the Senate as requests "copies of the charges, if any," in relation to Mr. Fitz, and in doing so must be distinctly understood as neither affirming nor denying that any such charges were made. . . .[30]

One of the recognized and fundamental powers of the Congress is to inquire into the operations of government as a *legislative* power. Presidents who have exercised and supported the executive privilege have not denied this as a proper congressional function. And the Supreme Court has agreed that inquiry into the departments of the executive branch *which is pertinent* is a proper function of the Congress.

In 1837, President Jackson faced a resolution which the House adopted to investigate the condition of the executive departments and which concerned their integrity and efficiency. Specifically the House wanted the president and the department heads to give information about appointments made during his administration which had not received the advice and consent of the Senate. Jackson's reply was:

> I shall on the one hand cause every possible facility con-

29. Ibid., p. 133.
30. Ibid., p. 134.

> sistent with law and justice to be given to the investigation of specific charges; and on the other shall repudiate all attempts to invade the just rights of the Executive Departments and of the individuals composing the same. . . .
>
> I shall repel all such attempts as an invasion of the principles of justice, as well as of the Constitution, and I shall esteem it my sacred duty to the people of the United States to resist them as I would the establishment of a Spanish Inquisition.[31]

Jackson may have been wrong.[32] The House allegation involved possible corruption or inefficiency, or waste. Jackson had removed an official from office, but the official had died by the time of the request. Thus, Jackson may have been concerned, as was Jefferson, with the fairness of an inquiry, and in Jackson's case, about a man who could not defend himself.[33]

One of the more unusual aspects of the development of the executive privilege came during the presidency of John Tyler. In this instance the House of Representatives found itself investigating its own members and sought to obtain information from the president in the course of a planned inquiry. On March 16, 1842, a resolution was adopted requesting that the president and department heads provide the names of House members who had, during the 26th and 27th Congresses, sought appointments to office.[34] A week later, Tyler wrote a firm denial and extended the denial to his department heads. He appears to have considered, as have later presidents, that his immediate subordinates constituted an integral part of the executive and were subject to his control. He must have

31. *Congressional Debates*, vol. 13, pt. 2, 1837, appendix, p. 202.

32. See *Watkins* v. *U.S.*, 354 U.S. 178, 187 (1957).

33. Richardson, *Messages and Papers of the Presidents*, 4:105–6. Jackson said he would permit department heads to answer requests if they chose, provided they did not "injure the public service by consuming their time and that of their subordinates."

34. A valuable analysis of this episode is found in Robert J. Morgan, *A Whig Embattled* (Lincoln: University of Nebraska Press, 1954), pp. 87 ff.

had the view expressed many years later by Woodrow Wilson that the cabinet is an executive, not a political, body.

Tyler said that the House request violated the executive right in two ways.

> All appointments to office made by a President become from the date of their nomination to the Senate official acts, which are matter of record and are at the proper time made known to the House of Representatives and to the country. But the applications for office, or letters respecting appointments, or conversations held with individuals on such subjects, are not official proceedings, and cannot by any means be made to partake of the character of official proceedings, unless after the nomination of such person so writing or conversing . . . the President shall think proper to lay such correspondence or conversations before the Senate.[35]

Not unlike some of his predecessors, Tyler based his refusal on the separation of powers.

> . . . it becomes me, in defense of the Constitution and laws of the United States, to protect the Executive department from all encroachment on its powers, rights and duties. In my judgment, a compliance with the resolution . . . would be a surrender of duties and powers which the Constitution has conferred *exclusively* on the Executive. . . . The appointing power, so far as it is bestowed on the President, is conferred without reserve or qualification. . . . I cannot perceive anywhere in the Constitution any right conferred on the House of Representatives to hear the reasons which an applicant may urge for an appointment to office under the Executive department, or any duty resting upon the House . . . by which it may become responsible for any such appointment.[36]

By this statement, Tyler emphasized that the appointing power is not exclusive with the president, but that the appointing power, "so far as it is bestowed on the President, is conferred without reserve or qualifications." The

35. Richardson, *Messages and Papers of the Presidents*, 4:105 ff.
36. Ibid. Emphasis supplied.

Constitution grants the president the power to "nominate" and he must share the appointing power with the Senate for those offices where the "advice and consent" is required.[37]

In his *Whig Embattled*, Robert J. Morgan considered the appointing power of a president as a right governed by executive privacy, one grounded on executive autonomy, and concluded that the House action directed to Tyler was an attempt to invade that privacy.[38] Although Tyler was adamant in his refusal, he did not indicate a blanket denial in a later House request for reports respecting the affairs of the Cherokee Indians and some alleged frauds. He wrote:

> . . . it is well settled . . . that . . . the head of a department cannot be compelled to produce any papers, or to disclose any transactions relating to the executive functions of the Government which he declares are confidential, or such as the public interest requires should not be divulged; and the persons who have been the channels of communication to officers of the State are in like manner protected from the disclosure of their names. Other instances of privileged communications might be enumerated, if it were deemed necessary. *These principles are as applicable to evidence sought by a legislature as to that required by a court.*[39]

Although Tyler's position would not be fully supported

37. Tyler's recognition of this shared power is in contrast to the comment made by President Nixon in his letter of March 31, 1970, to Senator William B. Saxbe of Ohio in which he reaffirmed his support of his nomination of Judge G. Harold Carswell to the U.S. Supreme Court. The president wrote: "What is centrally at issue in this nomination is the constitutional responsibility of the President to *appoint* members of the Court—and whether this responsibility can be frustrated by those who wish to substitute their own philosophy or their own subjective judgment for that of the one person entrusted by the Constitution with the power of *appointment*" (*Congressional Record,* 91st Cong., 2d sess., p. 10158; emphasis supplied).

38. Morgan, *A Whig Embattled*, p. 88.

39. Asher C. Hinds, *Hinds' Precedents of the House of Representatives of the United States* (Washington, D.C.: U.S. Government Printing Office, 1907), 3:182. Emphasis supplied.

now by the courts, he denied that the Congress had unrestricted power to cause the production of papers and documents.[40] He also employed the phrase "the public interest" and associated that interest with the fairness doctrine emphasized by Jefferson. If information collected were disseminated, not only would such disclosure not be in the public interest, it would be grossly unjust to those involved. His main objection was that for him to comply would be an interference with executive discretion. But his defense was not for total exclusion.

> . . . The injunction of the Constitution that the President "shall take care that the laws be faithfully executed," necessarily confers an authority, commensurate with the obligation imposed, to inquire into the manner in which all public agents perform the duties assigned to them by law. To be effective, these inquiries must often be confidential. They may result in the collection of truth and falsehood; or they may be incomplete, and may require further prosecution. To maintain that the President can exercise no discretion after the time in which the matters thus collected shall be promulgated, or in respect to the character of the information obtained, would deprive him at once of the means of performing one of the most salutary duties of his office. . . . To require from the Executive the transfer of this discretion to a coordinate branch of the Government is equivalent to the denial of its possession by him and would render him dependent upon that branch in the performance of a duty purely executive.[41]

Tyler later sent some information, but he did not include commentary about individuals which he thought, in his discretion, would be unjust to them.

It is significant to note that Tyler chose also to base

40. Tyler's position on control over information in the executive branch generally has since been made much more restrictive. See *U.S. ex rel Touhy* v. *Ragan,* 340 U.S. 462 (1950) and *McGrain* v. *Daugherty,* 273 U.S. 135 (1927).

41. Hinds, *Hinds' Precedents,* 3:181.

his refusal on the ground that the requested papers and documents would not be of aid to the Congress in fulfilling its legislative function, one of the first occasions a president based the executive privilege on the "need to know" claimed by the Congress.[42]

The extent to which a president can control information took on a different direction under the administration of Tyler's successor, James K. Polk. The question, essentially, was whether Polk was obliged to deliver up requested papers about events which occurred during Tyler's presidency. The request by the House of Representatives called for papers which would cover certain payments for some activities of the Department of State during Daniel Webster's tenure as secretary. Polk's message stated that the expenses involved covered activities authorized by statute and that the president was privileged to settle the expenses annually with accounting officials. Tyler could have made them public had he wanted to do so, but he did not. Expenditures of the kind involved, Polk stated, had not before been made public, and they had thereby been given a seal of "confidence" by his predecessor. Said Polk:

> An important question arises, whether a subsequent President, either voluntarily or at the request of one branch of Congress, can without a violation of the spirit of the law revise the acts of his predecessor and expose to public view that which he had determined should not be "made public." If not a matter of strict duty, it would certainly be a safe general rule that this should not be done. Indeed, it may well happen, and probably would happen, that the President for the time being would not be in possession of the information upon which his predecessor acted, and could not, therefore, have the means of judging whether he had exercised wisely or not.[43]

In Polk's view, when a president leaves office there is an end to the things he did and his successor cannot prop-

42. Wiggins, "Government Operations," p. 83.

43. Richardson, *Messages and Papers of the Presidents*, 4:433.

erly be called upon to explain what he did. Polk did not argue that records of these kinds were completely beyond the reach of the Congress. The statute could be changed, a prudent action or not. But he left open the question whether a president might deny some information because of his primacy in foreign affairs.

The next instance in this review of the development of the executive privilege came during the administration of President James Buchanan. On March 28, 1860, Buchanan sent a message of protest to the House of Representatives in response to its resolution that a committee inquire into whether the president or any other officer of the government, had, from use of money or patronage "or other improper means" sought to influence the Congress in legislation affecting the states or territories. In what may be one of the longest sentences from a president to the Congress, Buchanan replied, in part, as follows:

> I . . . solemnly protest against these proceedings of the House of Representatives, because they are in violation of the rights of the coordinate executive branch of the Government and subversive of its constitutional independence; because they are calculated to foster a band of interested parasites and informers, ever ready, for their own advantage, to swear before *ex parte* committees to pretended private conversations between the President and themselves, incapable from their nature of being disproved, thus furnishing material for harassing him, degrading him in the eyes of the country, and eventually, should he be a weak or timid man, rendering him subservient to improper influences in order to avoid such prosecutions and annoyances; because they tend to destroy that harmonious action for the common good which ought to be maintained, and which I sincerely desire to cherish, between coordinate branches of the Government; and finally, because, if unresisted, they would establish a precedent dangerous and embarrassing to all my successors, to whatever political party they might be attached.[44]

44. Ibid., 5:618–19.

Buchanan thus detailed his views about the separation of powers and reasons why a president and his close associates should not be subject to congressional demands for information, certainly not discourse which may have taken place between a president and "any other officer of the government." But as will be considered later, he echoed Tyler's sentiments about a right of executive privacy.

When President Ulysses S. Grant was asked for a reply to a House resolution requesting information about acts which may have been performed away from the seat of government, his denial was forceful. There was nothing, he said, in the Constitution which gave the House authority to require him to account for the conduct of his purely executive duties. But he did not support, apparently, a blanket claim to executive privilege. Two areas in which the House had jurisdiction might possibly be warranted: the discharge of proper legislative functions and impeachment proceedings. But since these two areas of House authority were not involved in the resolution, Grant said he would not comply. He presented yet another reason, perhaps introduced for the first time by a president in claiming executive privilege. He said that the House was violating a constitutional guarantee "which protects every citizen, the President as well as the humblest in the land, from being made a witness against himself."[45]

Grant seemed most irritated over the House question about performing his duties away from Washington. "No act of Congress can limit, suspend, or confine this constitutional duty. I am not aware of the existence of any act of Congress which assumes thus to limit or restrict the exercise of the functions of the Executive. *Were there such acts, I should nevertheless recognize the superior authority of the Constitution, and should exercise the powers required thereby of the President*."[46]

45. Ibid., 7:362.

46. Ibid., p. 363. Emphasis supplied. Grant had spent some of the hot summer months away from Washington.

What has been considered one of the greatest debates to that time between the Senate and a president over the executive privilege came during President Grover Cleveland's tenure. Following a long period when the Republican party had a majority in the Congress and occupied the White House, Cleveland, a Democrat, came into office in 1885. The House of Representatives had a Democratic majority, but the Senate remained Republican in its majority. After coming into office, Cleveland removed several hundred persons from positions in the executive branch over the raging protests of members of the Congress. Requests were frequent during 1886 to department heads for papers involving the *reasons* for the removals. Cleveland directed these department heads not to comply and said that the denials were based on two factors, the *public interest*, and the fact that the papers requested related to purely *executive functions*.

The Senate claimed that the Congress had created the offices in question and for that reason it had a right to information concerning those persons who filled them and the circumstances surrounding the removals. In one instance, the Senate denounced the attorney general for refusing to provide information about the suspension of the U.S. attorney for Alabama. Cleveland had appointed someone else to the post and sent his name to the Senate for confirmation. The Senate Committee on the Judiciary asked for information concerning both the removal and the proposed appointment. The former was not sent.[47]

The question posed from this last episode has continued since that day. Is it within the constitutional power of either house of the Congress to have access to executive papers and documents relating to the public offices created by the statutes of the Congress?[48]

47. Rogers, *Memorandums*, 1958, pp. 14, 16. Also, Richardson, *Messages and Papers of the Presidents*, 8:378, 379, 381.

48. It was not until 1926, in *Myers* v. *U.S.*, op cit., that a judicial entry was made on the power of the president to remove persons he

The president is granted authority by the Constitution to take "care that the laws be faithfully executed." If he is to do this he must have assistants. These assistants must be of his own choosing if he is in a position to make them an arm of the president and thereby dominate them. He cannot do this if he does not have the power also to remove them should he want to do so for any reason, whether for unwillingness to follow his directions or for being otherwise unsuited, in his opinion. What is unusual in the issue between Cleveland and the Senate is that he stated he could have destroyed the papers or taken them for his personal use, thereby putting them beyond the call of the Senate.[49] Furthermore, if the papers were to be submitted, they would have to be only those papers "official" in nature and not *all* papers merely because they were in the files of an executive department.

Cleveland's comment was, in part, as follows:

> The requests and demands which by the score have for nearly three months been presented to the different departments of the Government, whatever may be their form, have but one complexion. They assume the right of the Senate to sit in judgment upon the exercise of my exclusive discretion and Executive function, for which I am solely responsi-

had appointed to office. Two later decisions bear also on the subject, *Humphrey's Executor* v. *U.S.*, 295 U.S. 602 (1935), and *Wiener* v. *U.S.*, 357 U.S. 349 (1958). Presumably Cleveland's stand would have been sustained had it been tested at the time.

49. The following interchange took place during the 1971 hearing:

> PROFESSOR WINTER. I take it Congressman, that you disagree with what I thought to be the established tradition that the papers of the President are his personal property.
>
> REPRESENTATIVE MOSS. We have never even decided that. And I think again the Congress has a right to decide whether the papers of the President are his personal property until we passed the Presidential Librarian Act there was no provision to assist the President in taking care of his papers. But we did not settle the question of who owns or controls the papers of the President. [Senate, *Hearing*, 1971, p. 337]

> ble to the people from whom I have so lately received the sacred trust of office.[50]

Cleveland's position, acknowledged at least tacitly, was supported by Senate confirmation of the questioned appointee and indicates that the executive privilege can be extended to papers and documents which are not directly related to a constitutional or statutory requirement about the performance of the duties of the executive branch. But who determines the character of these papers and documents? Cleveland said the president does.

When President Theodore Roosevelt was met with a Senate resolution for information about some proceedings involving his attorney general, he said he would give

> the information in the possession of the executive department which appears to me to be material or relevant, on the subject of the resolution. I feel bound, however, to add that I have instructed the Attorney General not to respond to that portion of the resolution which calls for a statement of his reason for nonaction. I have done so because I do not conceive it to be within the authority of the Senate to give direction of this character to the head of an executive department, or to demand from him reasons for his action. Heads of the executive departments are subject to the Constitution, and to the laws passed by the Congress in pursuance of the Constitution, and to the directions of the President of the United States, but to no other direction whatever.[51]

Believing that it could not obtain what it wanted from the attorney general, the Senate sought to obtain it from Herbert Knox Smith, the head of the Bureau of Corporations. When he, too, declined, he was advised to produce the documents or he would face imprisonment by direction of the Senate. This reaction by the Senate Committee on

50. Grover Cleveland, *Presidential Problems* (New York: Century Co., 1904), pp. 63, 64.

51. *Congressional Record*, 60th Cong., 2d sess., pp. 527–28.

the Judiciary may be the first to suggest such a severe course in the exercise of executive privilege. But being advised of this threat, Roosevelt directed Smith to turn over to the president all the papers in the case.

> I have those papers in my possession, and last night I informed Senator Clark of the Judiciary Committee what I had done. I told him also that the Senate should not have those papers and that Herbert Knox Smith had turned them over to me. The only way the Senate or the committee can get those papers now is through my impeachment, and I so informed Senator Clark last night.
>
> The Senator informed me that the Senate was only anxious to exercise its prerogatives and that if the papers were of such a nature that they should not be made public the committee was ready to endorse my views. But, as I say, it is just as well to take no chances with a man like Culberson, who is behind this thing, so I will retain those papers until the 3rd of March at least.[52]

Thus frustrated, the Senate took under consideration a resolution, not unlike some introduced many years later. That 1909 resolution took this form:

> That any and every public document, paper, or record, or copy thereof, on the files of any department of the Government, relating to any subject whatever over which Congress has any grant of power, jurisdiction, or control, under the Constitution, and any information relative thereto within the possession of the officers of the department, is subject to the call or inspection of the Senate for its use in the exercise of its constitutional powers and jurisdiction.[53]

The resolution was debated, but did not come to a final vote. Two positions which were presented during the debate are pertinent to any consideration of the develop-

52. Lawrence F. Abbott, *The Letters of Archibald Butt, Personal Aide to President Roosevelt* (New York: Doubleday, Page & Co., 1924), pp. 305, 306.

53. Senate Resolution 248, January 13, 1909, *Congressional Record*, 60th Cong., 2d sess., p. 839.

ment of the executive privilege. Questions posed about the investigatory powers of the Congress were answered years later, in part, particularly during the so-called McCarthy episodes. One question in 1909 was whether there was any law which compelled department heads to give information and papers to the Congress. This prompted Senator Jonathan P. Dolliver of Iowa to say, "What I want to know is, where Congress gets authority either out of the Constitution or the laws of the United States to order an executive department about like a servant."[54] The other question was that if there was a refusal to obey a congressional request, what effective punishment could be given out by the Congress? Assuming a law to authorize some action could be passed, then how could it be enforced effectively? There was probably no effective remedy prevailing during the episode with Cleveland in 1886 and probably not one in 1909.[55]

In 1881 the U.S. Supreme Court had said that neither house of the Congress possesses a "general power of making inquiry into the private affairs of the citizen"[56] and the power the Congress does possess is limited to inquiries relating to matters over which the particular house has jurisdiction and in which it may take other actions. The court said, in part:

> It is believed to be one of the chief merits of the American system of written constitutional law, that all the powers intrusted to government, whether State or national, are divided into three grand departments, the executive, the legislative, and the judicial. That the functions appropriate to each of these branches of government shall be vested in a separate body of public servants, and that the perfection of the system requires that the lines which separate and divide these departments shall be broadly and clearly

54. Ibid., p. 3732.

55. W. W. Willoughby, *The Constitutional Law of the United States*, 2d ed. (New York: Baker, Voorhis and Co., 1929).

56. *Kilbourn* v. *Thompson*, 103 U.S. 168.

defined. It is also essential to the successful working of this system that the persons intrusted with power in any one of these branches shall not be permitted to encroach upon the powers confided to the others, but that each shall by law of its creation be limited to the exercise of powers appropriate to its own department and no other.

... It also remains true, as a general rule, that the powers confided by the Constitution to one of these departments cannot be exercised by another.[57]

In 1897, in *Chapman*, the court established the proposition that to make an investigation lawful it was not necessary that the resolution should declare in advance what the Senate "meditated doing when the investigation was concluded."[58]

The next significant situation concerning the executive privilege came in 1924 when the Senate passed a resolution for the appointment of a committee to inquire into the Bureau of Internal Revenue and gave the committee the authority to subpoena witnesses. In a letter of April 10, 1924, the committee wrote Secretary of the Treasury Andrew Mellon for information about all companies in which he had an interest. Apparently the object was to investigate those companies.

The next day, on April 11, President Calvin Coolidge sent a special message to the Senate saying that the information requested of Mellon would be refused, and he based his refusal on the ground of "law and custom" and that to reveal it would be detrimental to the public interest. The president observed that it was quite proper for the Senate to engage in partisan political criticism, but he objected to the inquiry at hand in these words:

I recognize ... that it is perfectly legitimate for the Senate to indulge in political discussion and partisan criticism. But the attack which is being made on the Treasury Department

57. Ibid., 191, 192.

58. *In re Chapman*, 166 U.S. 661, 670.

> goes beyond any of these legitimate requirements. Seemingly the request for a list of the companies in which the Secretary of the Treasury was alleged to be interested, for the purposes of investigating their tax returns, must have been dictated by some other motive than a desire to secure information for the pupose of legislation. . . .
>
> The constitutional and legal rights of the Senate ought to be maintained at all times. Also the same must be said of the executive departments. But these rights ought not to be used as a subterfuge to cover unwarranted intrusion. It is the duty of the Executive to resist such intrusion and to bring to the attention of the Senate its serious consequences. That I shall do in this instance.[59]

During the debate in the Senate on the matter, Senator Joseph T. Robinson of Arkansas observed:

> The President, of course, and the Secretary of the Treasury, subordinate to him, may refuse to submit to the Senate any information sought of the Executive to maintain secrecy. If there are records in the Treasury Department which the Executive is entitled to seal with secrecy from a coordinate branch of the Government there is no disposition on this side of the Chamber to interfere with the exercise of his prerogative in that or any other particular.[60]

Six years later, on June 6, 1930, Secretary of State Henry L. Stimson replied to a request from the Senate Committee on Foreign Relations about some confidential telegrams and letters relating to the London Conference and proposed treaty. The tenor of Stimson's reply was to answer the questions he thought appropriate to Senate consideration of the treaty, but no more. He refused to divulge some of the papers called for because President Herbert C. Hoover directed him not to do so, claiming it would not be in the public interest to have them released to the committee. The reaction from the committee was

59. *Congressional Record*, 68th Cong., 1st sess., p. 6087.
60. Ibid., p. 6103.

in the form of a resolution claiming that as a part of the Senate's function in the ratification of a treaty it should have access to all facts which "entered into the antecedent or attendant negotiations of any treaty," and that the committee had a right to full and free access to all records involved in negotiations.

The treaty-making power is one of the shared powers. But the president and the president alone has the power to negotiate; the Senate has the sole power to ratify, enter conditions or reservations, or not to ratify at all. The Senate's position was that to ratify responsibly it needed all information available so it would know how the provisions of the treaty were arrived at, and that in so asking it was not impinging on any executive authority. It insisted also that it was not entering the arena at the stage of the negotiations; it merely wanted the information used to convince the president to conclude the treaty recommendation.

In his letter to Senator William E. Borah, chairman of the committee, Stimson said:

> There have been no concealed understandings on this matter, nor are there any commitments whatever except as appear in the treaty itself and the interpretative exchange of notes recently suggested by your committee, all of which are now in the hands of the Senate. Respecting the other papers called for, I am directed by the President to say that their production would not in his opinion be compatible with the public interest. These requests call for the production and possible publication of informal and confidential conversations, communications, and tentative suggestions of a kind which are common to almost every negotiation and without which such negotiations can not be successfully carried on. If the confidence in which they were made to the American delegation in London is broken, it would materially impair the possibility of future successful negotiations between this Government and other nations.[61]

61. *Congressional Record*, 71st Cong., 2d sess., p. 12029.

Later at its special session to consider ratification of the treaty, Senator George W. Norris of Nebraska observed: "I do not want to look into these secret documents and go through them so far as any curiosity of my own is concerned, but we are called upon here under the Constitution to perform a governmental function which is extremely important and always is in the making of a treaty."[62]

Hoover's reply to this challenge from the Senate came in his message of July 11, 1930. In it he said there were many informal statements and reports given to the United States in confidence, and it was his duty, in order to maintain amicable relations with other nations, not to publicize all negotiations and statements which went into the making of a treaty. To do so would mean he had violated the trust of the nations involved and "the invariable practice of nations."[63] The United States had no other choice but observe those considerations and retain the confidence which was given. Furthermore, the United States entered into these relations knowing what its conduct would have to be and the Senate should have known it.

He concluded, in part, as follows:

> . . . No Senator has been refused an opportunity to see the confidential material referred to, provided only he will agree to receive and hold the same in the confidence in which it has been received and held by the Executive. A number of Senators have availed themselves of this opportunity. I believe that no Senator can read these documents without agreeing with me that no other course than to insist upon the maintenance of such confidence is possible. . . .
>
> In view of this, I believe that to further comply with the above resolution would be incompatible with the public interest.[64]

One of the more unusual developments regarding executive control over information came during President

62. *Congressional Record*, Special Session of the Senate, 1930, p. 362.
63. Ibid., pp. 108, 109.
64. Ibid.

Franklin D. Roosevelt's first term. It is similar to the issue raised over Andrew Jackson's refusal to provide the Senate with a copy of a paper he had sent to the heads of departments. In Roosevelt's case, however, the call was to provide the speaker of the House with a full transcript of his press conference of May 3, 1935. The president declined to do so, saying, in part, "I do not believe, however, that it would be advisable for me to create the precedent of sending to the Congress for documentary use the text of remarks I make at the bi-weekly conferences with the newspaper representatives here in Washington."To do so, he said, would mean that he could not speak informally and would bring about a consciousness of restraint as well as the necessity for constant preparation of his remarks.[65] What a contrast to news conferences by later presidents!

In a 1941 House inquiry by the Committee on Naval Affairs, a request was made that the Federal Bureau of Investigation provide it with reports and correspondence concerning investigations made by that agency in connection with labor disturbances in industrial establishments which had naval contracts. The request was denied. Attorney General Robert H. Jackson said that a number of requests had been received from committees of the Congress and compliance was not practicable since many of the requests were comprehensive in character. In an Opinion, Jackson stated:

> It is the position of this Department, restated now with the approval and at the direction of the President, that all investigative reports are confidential documents of the executive departments of the Government, to aid in the duty laid upon the President by the Constitution to "take care that the laws be faithfully executed," and that congressional or public access to them would not be in the public interest.[66]

65. *Congressional Record*, 74th Cong., 1st sess., pp. 7002, 7186. The text of Roosevelt's letter is included in the Appendix, sec. II.

66. *Official Opinions of the Attorneys General of the United States* (Washington, D.C.: U.S. Government Printing Office, 1949), 40:46.

Jackson also insisted that disclosure would prejudice law enforcement; that disclosure would be prejudicial to the national interest and seriously and adversely affect the usefulness of the FBI. He expressed concern that injustices might result to innocent persons because of the statements contained in some of the reports from persons who had malicious intent or were misinformed.

Later, on January 20, 1944, a Select House Committee to Investigate the Federal Communications Commission convened to hear testimony from J. Edgar Hoover, director of the FBI. Hoover had been served with a subpoena and he honored it with an appearance. But the committee was met with a firm denial for information of any kind. He was not asked to produce any documentary evidence, but rather was shown some letters, which he refused to admit he had received in the performance of his official duties. The following colloquy occurred:

> MR. GAREY [committee counsel]. You were asked at the last hearing to produce before this committee the written directive which you had received from the President of the United States respecting the scope of the testimony which you were not to give, putting it one way, or which you would be permitted to give, before this committee. Are you now ready to produce that written directive?
>
> MR. HOOVER. I am not.[67]

This prompted the committee chairman to give qualified recognition to the president's control over information.

> . . . Under this general question of the right of the witness to refuse to testify, we have a situation when the law seems to be rather indefinite, but for over 140 years a certain exemption has been granted to the executive departments, particularly where it involves military secrets or relations

67. U.S. Congress, House of Representatives, *Hearings of the Select Committee to Investigate the Federal Communications Commission*, 78th Cong., 2d sess., 1944, p. 2337. See also the attorney general's letter in the Appendix, sec. III.

> with foreign nations. Yet we, of course, realize that the President, by a blanket order, could not exempt a witness who is an official in an executive department, I take it, from the duty of testifying when properly called before a committee like this one, with authority.

This was a specific indication of proper executive control over information if it involved military secrets and foreign relations, but presumably *only* if asserted personally by the president on a case-by-case basis.

When a request was made through a subpoena to Harold D. Smith, the director of the Bureau of the Budget, to produce files concerning the transfer of the functions of the Radio Intelligence Division of the Federal Communications Commission, the request by the committee was denied. Later, the chairman of the FCC was subpoened to appear and answer questions, and he, too, refused. Each was told by the president not to testify because to do so would not be in the public interest.[68]

On August 28, 1945, President Truman directed that the secretaries of state, war, and the Navy, the attorney general, the Joint Chiefs of Staff, and the directors of the Bureau of the Budget and the Office of War Information take steps to prevent the public release, except with his approval, of information concerning the Cryptanalytic Unit. Shortly thereafter, a joint congressional committee was authorized to investigate the attack on Pearl Harbor. It had been preceded by seven other such inquiries. The president later advised the chairman of the committee, Senator Alben W. Barkley of Kentucky, on October 23, 1945, that he had arranged that the files of the White House be made available to the committee, and that he, the president, should be advised if there was any problem of "complete access." On November 7, 1945, however, the president said that information should be given, provided

68. *Congressional Record,* 78th Cong., 2d sess., appendix, pp. 1034, 1066.

that it did not "include any files or written material."[69]

This limitation presumably meant that files or written material could not be removed, but information from them could be transcribed. The basic restriction was that whatever was disclosed had to be *pertinent* to the inquiry. The first instruction was clear, the second discretionary to those supervising access to the records. This arrangement was not agreeable to the members of the committee, but the president remained firm in his qualified denial.

During the two Eisenhower administrations, 1953–61, a series of issues arose which involved varying degrees of presidential control over information. The most significant came in 1954 when the president issued his directive of May 17, cited above, intended to restrict individuals in the executive branch from giving testimony before the subcommittee of the Senate Committee on Government Operations. This directive was used extensively by subordinates as a claim of authority to withhold information about government activities. The effect of it was the same as a blanket order even though it was originally issued to cover defense matters only. It is not evident that the president was involved personally in directing many of these denials, which should be considered, for the most part, in the category of subordinate claims of privilege, not the executive privilege exercised solely by the president, formally or not.[70]

At a news conference on August 17, 1954, Eisenhower said in reply to a question about the controversial Dixon-Yates issue that "any one of you here present may, singly or in an investigation group, go to the Bureau of the Budget, to the chief of the Atomic Energy Commission, and

69. Rogers, *Memorandums*, 1958, p. 28.

70. A detailed review of the exercise of executive privilege and of informational withholding by the executive branch is in Robert Kramer and Herman Marcuse, "Executive Privilege—A Study of the Period 1953–1960," *George Washington Law Review* 29, no. 4 (April 1961): 623, no. 5 (June 1961): 827.

get the complete record from the inception of the idea to this very minute, and it is all yours."[71]

But during the proceedings before the 1955 Senate Committee on Interstate and Foreign Commerce on the nomination of Admiral Lewis Strauss to be Secretary of Commerce, an effort was made to solicit from Strauss information about the Dixon-Yates affair since it involved the Atomic Energy Commission, of which he was then chairman. He declined to give information on the ground that it was confidential and although he did not himself claim privilege he said to reveal it would violate the separation of powers. The information, he said, was a matter of conversations between himself and the president and only the president could waive the confidence. This reaction has the element of executive privacy which is considered later, but bears on the development of the executive privilege by reason of a reference to a claim on the doctrine of the separation of powers.[72]

In 1956, during consideration in the Congress of the Mutual Security Act, an amendment was offered similar to the 1909 resolution directed to Theodore Roosevelt. The 1956 proposal would have required "any officer or employee of the Government having information, or having custody of documents or other data, relating to the programs being administered under this act, shall promptly furnish any such information, documents or other data."[73]

The proposal was defeated, but was renewed the following year. It took this form:

> Any Government agency shall furnish any information requested by any such committee with respect to the activities and responsibilities of that agency under this act

71. *Public Papers of the Presidents of the United States: Dwight D. Eisenhower* (Washington, D.C.: U.S. Government Printing Office, 1960), p. 199.

72. Strauss was not confirmed as secretary.

73. *Congressional Record*, 84th Cong., 2d sess., p. 11382.

> and it shall be the duty of any officer or employee of the Government having information relating to programs being administered under this act to furnish promptly to such committee or committees, upon request by any such committees, full information with respect to such activities and responsibilities.[74]

Would the amendment, if adopted, constitute a waiver of executive privilege? To what extent would the security of the United States be adversely affected? Senator Joseph C. O'Mahoney of Wyoming explained that if enacted, the amendment "would constitute a waiver of executive privilege by any subordinate of the President, unless the President himself exercises his privilege." This is a recognition of the executive privilege, but only if exercised by the president. The senator then said:

> It is generally agreed that the President has the constitutional right, in matters of foreign relations, to decline to give out information when he believes that such information would impair the national security. I am not dealing with that matter at all. A statute could not overrule a constitutional right.
>
> But where, as we know in this case, the power that we grant to the President must be exercised by subordinate officials who never see the President, then I want to be certain that the executive privilege is not extended to such persons . . .
>
> I do not think it would constitute a waiver of the President's executive privilege; no.[75]

This recognition of the constitutional basis for the executive privilege in this informal manner is but indicative of some congressional reactions to its exercise. Although the amendment was defeated by a vote of fifty-five to thirty-one, had it been enacted and observed, it would have meant, very probably, that some subordinates "who never see the President" might well begin seeing him.

74. *Congressional Record*, 85th Cong., 1st sess., p. 9147.
75. Ibid., p. 9148.

Senator Homer C. Capehart of Indiana, who opposed the amendment, said that "orderly government" will cease if "Congress can call before it any disgruntled employee of the executive department, who will be able to say whatever he pleases." And somewhat contrary to some of his more recent views, Senator Fulbright observed that "one branch must, occasionally, accord to the other branch a certain degree of trust. . . . If we are to be fully informed, then I suppose we should take the responsiblity of administering the law day by day. It is a wholly unworkable approach to this problem."[76]

In the course of an inquiry into the operations in Vietnam in 1959, the acting director of the International Cooperation Administration declined to submit evaluation reports which had been made for the agency, and he said the decision was not limited to evaluation reports in Vietnam, but the denial applied to such reports made on any country. This prompted Senator Wayne Morse of Oregon to say:

> My record for 15 years shows that I have always defended any administration in its right to exercise that doctrine [of executive privilege], and shall continue to do so, because as an old teacher of this constitutional principle, I couldn't possibly deny and wouldn't want to, this right of exercise to any President.
>
> But I am sure you are also aware that the exercise of the right of the doctrine of executive privilege is purely discretionary on the part of the President, and when a President, in effect, makes it a blanket policy, then it rightly becomes a matter of public policy issue for the people of this country to judge as to whether the President seeks to invoke government by secrecy upon a free people by taking a discretionary right and turning it into a uniform practice.[77]

76. Ibid., p. 9150.

77. U.S. Congress, Senate, *Situation in Vietnam: Hearings before the Subcommittee on State Department Organization and Public Affairs of the Committee on Foreign Relations*, 86th Cong., 1st sess., 1959, p. 129.

Morse's position was that the executive privilege has a constitutional base, but it must be exercised by a president in particular cases, not as a general rule.

During these 1959 inquiries, the acting director of ICA was asked by Senator Hennings: "Do you feel that you individually as an officer, in your capacity as administrator, are invested with executive privilege . . . ?"[78] The reply was in the affirmative. When, later, James W. Riddleberger assumed the directorship, he was questioned about withholding information and the claim of executive privilege. He said: "Within my powers, I shall not withhold facts, no matter how damaging they may be. I shall assume personal responsibility for all decisions which I make, but I shall treat as privileged the judgments and recommendations of my staff which were considered in reaching my decisions."[79] Again, this is a subordinate claim of privilege which Senator Morse denied he could support. The response by Riddleberger, however, was that "judgments and recommendations of my staff" were protected. This remains at the core of the executive privilege, and efforts to force disclosure of judgments and recommendations are strongly resisted by presidents.

During his news conference on July 1, 1959, President Eisenhower said that there was some concern in the Congress about the claims of privilege, especially during the ICA investigations, where it was believed that the "executive branch had misused the claim of Executive privilege and denied them information they feel they should have." He elaborated his position in this way:

> Well, there are certain things, particularly in the security field that, if you reveal, are very obviously damaging the

78. U.S. Congress, Senate, *Executive Privilege (ICA): Hearings before the Subcommittee on Constitutional Rights of the Senate Committee on the Judiciary*, 86th Cong., 1st sess., 1959, pt. 2, p. 355.

79. U.S. Congress, Senate, *Mutual Security Appropriations for 1960 (and Related Agencies): Hearings before the Committee on Appropriations*, 86th Cong., 1st sess., 1959, p. 132.

> United States and I think anyone of good sense will see that. And you simply must take measures to see that those things are not revealed.
>
> For example, suppose you have a method of getting information. Now that particular information can be obtained only in one way. Therefore you reveal it. Instantly, you can topple an entire system of getting information. So, there are all sorts of things that simply cannot be revealed.
>
> There is nothing new about this. . . . But, I am using my own conscience on the matter and when such things as these come to me for decision, I shall continue to do so.[80]

During the 1971 hearing, this question was raised: "I wonder how many times the President has invoked the executive privilege over the last few years?" Senator Fulbright replied: "My staff tells me he thinks only once by Mr. Nixon and prior to that the last invocation was by Mr. Eisenhower. I know of no other instance."[81]

The privilege was exercised on February 8, 1962, however, when President John F. Kennedy wrote to Secretary of Defense Robert S. McNamara, and directed him to refuse to provide certain information to a Senate subcommittee.[82]

One week later, on February 15, 1962, Representative John E. Moss of California, chairman of the Special Government Information Subcommittee of the Committee on Government Operations, wrote the president, in part, as follows:

> Dear Mr. President:
>
> In your letter of February 8, 1962 to Secretary McNamara you directed him to refuse certain information to a Senate Subcommittee. The concluding paragraph of your letter stated:
>
> "The principle which is at stake here cannot be auto-

80. *Public Papers*, 1959, p. 489.
81. Senate, *Hearing*, 1971, p. 209.
82. Ibid., p. 33.

matically applied to every request for information. Each case must be judged on its merits."

A similar letter from President Eisenhower on May 17, 1954 also refused information to a Senate Subcommittee, setting forth the same arguments covered in your letter. President Eisenhower did not, however, state that future questions of availability of information to the Congress would have to be answered as they came up.

I know you are aware of the result of President Eisenhower's letter. Time after time Executive branch employees far down the administrative line from the President fell back on his letter of May 17, 1954 as authority to withhold information from the Congress and the public.

. . . A Subcommittee staff study indicates that during the year between the time you took office and February 8, 1962, the claim of an "executive privilege" to withhold government information was not used successfully once, compared to the dozens of times in previous years administrative employees held up "executive privilege" as a shield against public and Congressional access to information.[83]

Kennedy's response on March 7, 1962, was the forerunner of expressions by his successors on the claim of executive privilege. He wrote Moss as follows:

Dear Mr. Chairman:

This is in reply to your letter of last month inquiring generally about the practice this administration will follow in invoking the doctrine of executive privilege in withholding certain information from the Congress.

As your letter indicated, my letter of February 8 to Secretary McNamara made it perfectly clear that the directive to refuse to make certain specific information available to a special subcommittee of the Senate Armed Services Committee was limited to that specific request and that "each case must be judged on its merits."

As you know, this Administration has gone to great lengths to achieve full cooperation with the Congress in mak-

83. Ibid., pp. 33, 34. The full text of the correspondence between Moss and Kennedy is included in the Appendix, sec. V.

> ing available to it all appropriate documents, correspondence and information. That is the basic policy of this Administration, and it will continue to be so. Executive privilege can be invoked only by the President and will not be used without specific Presidential approval. Your own interest in assuring the widest public accessibility to governmental information, is, of course, well known, and I can assure you this Administration will continue to cooperate with your subcommittee and the entire Congress in achieving this objective.[84]

The extent to which Kennedy invoked executive privilege is difficult to ascertain. The Library of Congress Congressional Research Service reported on May 25, 1972, a series of instances in which information had been withheld and testimony refused, but there is no clear indication from this report whether the president directed these refusals or whether they were done under his directive of March 7, 1962.[85]

Representative Moss directed a letter to President Johnson on March 31, 1965, inquiring about the exercise of the executive privilege. His reply came on April 2, 1965.

> Dear Mr. Chairman:
>
> I have your recent letter discussing the use of the claim of "executive privilege" in connection with Congressional requests for documents and other information.
>
> Since assuming the Presidency, I have followed the policy laid down by President Kennedy in his letter to you of March 7, 1962, dealing with this subject. Thus, the claim of "executive privilege" will continue to be made only by the President. . . .[86]

The executive privilege was not an issue with Johnson and the Congress. Presumably his relations with the Con-

84. Ibid., p. 34.

85. Several of the examples are obviously claims of subordinate privilege. In March, 1973, the listing was amended and included also a series of alleged uses of executive privilege by President Nixon. See *Congressional Record*, 93rd Cong., 1st sess., pp. H2242–46.

86. Senate, *Hearing*, 1971, p. 35.

gress were such that information wanted was provided in some way, either released with agreed-upon restrictions or some accommodation was reached among those involved in both branches. He invoked executive privilege at least once, however, and this at the time of consideration of the nomination of Justice Abe Fortas to be the chief justice of the United States. This use of executive privilege more directly involves executive privacy and will be considered in Chapter V.

Eight days after his inauguration as president, Richard M. Nixon received the then familiar letter from Representative Moss. The Moss letter concluded with these words: "In view of the urgent need to safeguard and maintain a free flow of information to the Congress, I hope you will favorably consider a reaffirmation of the policy which provides, in essence, that the claim of 'executive privilege' will be invoked only by the President."[87]

The president's reply on April 7, 1969, was, in part, as follows:

> Knowing of your interest, I am sending you a copy of a memorandum I have issued to the heads of executive departments and agencies spelling out the procedural steps to govern the invocation of "executive privilege" under this Administration.
>
> As you well know, the claim of executive privilege has been the subject of much debate since George Washington first declared that a Chief Executive must "exercise discretion."
>
> I believe, and I have stated earlier, that the scope of executive privilege must be very narrowly construed. Under this Administration, executive privilege will not be asserted without specific Presidential approval.[88]

President Nixon stated on March 12, 1973, that he had invoked the executive privilege three times during his first term. These were the 1970 refusal to comply with the request by the House Government Operations Subcommit-

87. Ibid.
88. Ibid., p. 36.

tee on Intergovernmental Relations for FBI reports, the 1971 denial for projected military assistance plans, and the 1972 request for internal working papers about the U.S. Information Agency. This limited use of the executive privilege may be debated. The 1971 and 1972 hearings in both the House and the Senate indicate that numerous requests for testimony, for example, from Secretary Rogers or Henry Kissinger were either ignored or refused and are considered by critics of the executive privilege as having had the protection of the knowledge and consent of the president.[89]

Nearly twenty years after Harry S. Truman wrote his forceful refusal to honor a subpoena and appear before a congressional committee, Richard M. Nixon issued a statement on March 12, 1973, outlining his position on the executive privilege. It was prompted at the time by the demands that White House counsel John W. Dean III testify before the Senate Committee on the Judiciary about the fitness of L. Patrick Gray III to be the director of the Federal Bureau of Investigation. The president had stated earlier that he would not permit his aides to testify before congressional committees. He indicated in his public statement that he would rely on certain guidelines in invoking the executive privilege.[90] The executive privilege would not be invoked until "the compelling need for its exercise has been clearly demonstrated . . . and the request approved first by the Attorney General and then by the President." Anyone holding a position in the Cabinet and also as a member of the president's personal staff "shall comply with any reasonable request" provided that "the performance of his duties will not be seriously impaired thereby." But not in his White House capacity. "If the official believes that the request raises a substantial question

89. See, for example, "This Week in Washington," *National Observer*, January 27, 1973.

90. The full text of the statement appears in the Appendix, sec. IX.

as to the need for invoking executive privilege, he shall comply with the procedures set forth in my memorandum of March 24, 1969."[91]

The third guideline stated that "a member or former member of the President's personal staff normally shall follow the well-established precedent and decline a request for a formal appearance before a committee of the Congress." This guideline was based on a long-standing position by several presidents that those serving as counselors or aides or who are otherwise on the personal staff of the president are in effect in roles extending the presidency.[92]

Although presidential aides may be considered as advisers to the president, they are referred to as "troubleshooters," as liaisons with the Congress, or in some negotiating capacity. They have also been given coordinating assignments which could place them in roles well beyond that of adviser. Early in 1973 President Nixon announced that three cabinet officers who were also given dual roles as White House aides would have their assignments involving human resources, natural resources, and community development coordinated by White House aide

91. The 1969 memorandum stated that certain procedural steps would be required of any agency head before executive privilege could be claimed. The attorney general would review the request and advise the president if he believed it should be denied. Otherwise, the information would be released. Gray's nomination was withdrawn and he later resigned as acting director of the FBI. White House counsel Dean also resigned following allegations of possible wrongdoing in activities during the 1972 presidential campaign.

92. On April 17, 1973, the president modified his position to permit his aides to testify. This was the result of an expanded inquiry by the Senate. Excerpts from the president's news conference are included in the Appendix, sec. XI, and show his modified stand. The modification came as an agreement was reached between the Senate leaders handling the inquiry and the president. It was in the form of Senate committee guidelines, which are included in the Appendix, sec. XII. If observed, presidential aides would be permitted to testify, but were restricted to those matters under investigation and also barred from responses about any conversations they had with the president.

John D. Ehrlichman. Ehrlichman was assigned to coordinate domestic affairs for the president. Although this announcement indicated no change in the relationships with the Congress, it was evident that the assignments would affect the relationships between the president and some members of his cabinet.[93]

In this review of the development of the executive privilege the thread of continuity is the doctrine of the separation of powers. That was the view expressed in Washington's time and it has continued with varying emphasis ever since.

Much of the development of the privilege has involved executive powers in matters of national security, defense, and foreign affairs. More recently, however, the privilege has been extended firmly into the *advice* privilege. Whatever positions are taken by presidents, there is nonetheless the practice of finding ways, formal or informal, with or without restrictions, to meet the competing demands which arise from the resulting controversies. Central to the criticisms of the executive privilege is the element of secrecy and the need for it. Secrecy is alleged to be little more, on occasion, than a political device used by presidents and their subordinates to avoid being asked questions which might produce embarrassing answers. When this charge is made, the conflicts may be more spirited than would otherwise be the case. Presidents, quite naturally, are normally not willing to permit embarrassment if they can avoid it.

Whatever the future development may be for the executive privilege, it is most probable that the Congress will continue to insist that what it asks is vital and necessary in shaping legislative policy and in pursuing its practiced

93. The roles of cabinet officer and presidential counselors are considered in Chapter V. Erlichman resigned from his White House position in April, 1973, following allegations of wrongdoing associated with the activities of the Committee to Re-Elect the President in 1972.

role of legislative oversight of administration. Accommodations between the Congress and the executive undoubtedly will continue as they have in the past, with each maintaining degrees of independence, one from the other.

IV

Congress and the Need to Know

In the controversial decision of *Watkins* v. *U.S.*, Chief Justice Earl Warren said:

> The power of the Congress to conduct investigations is inherent in the legislative process. That power is broad. It encompasses inquiries concerning the administration of existing laws as well as proposed or possibly needed statutes. It includes surveys of defects in our social, economic or political system for the purpose of enabling the Congress to remedy them. It comprehends probes into departments of the Federal Government to expose corruption, inefficiency or waste. But broad as is this power of inquiry, it is not unlimited. . . . No inquiry is an end in itself; it must be related to and in furtherance of a legitimate task of the Congress.[1]

The matter before the court in this case involved alleged abuses of the investigatory power of the Congress "solely for the personal aggrandizement of the investigators or to 'punish' those investigated."

Thirty years earlier, Justice Willis Van Devanter wrote on the subject in *McGrain* v. *Daugherty* that "in actual legislative practice power to secure needed information" by

1. Op. cit., 187.

compelling witnesses to testify "has long been treated as an attribute of the power to legislate." But he also stated that investigations must aid in legislation, or have a valid legislative purpose.[2]

The Congress must have broad power to seek information and obtain testimony in the search for public policy. There is ample evidence that it has the power to compel testimony, that it needs even opinions if it is to fulfill its legitimate tasks. The fundamental question, however, is whether that power is so extensive, so unlimited, so absolute, so essential, and so vital that few restraints prevail on that power. There are restraints, and the most commonly observed is self-restraint and rational decisions that some inquiries should not extend beyond that which is pertinent to the legislative task. It must be recognized, however, that members of the Congress, generally, are jealous of their prerogatives. When they want information, they want it, and if it appears the only source is from individuals in the executive branch, they firmly believe it should be forthcoming. Senator John L. McClellan of Arkansas once complained to the Senate:

> . . . I have had some unhappy experiences in trying to get from the executive branch of the Government information which was considered pertinent and vital, and which would have provided information for the Congress which it should have in the performance of its legislative function. Some of the documents have been withheld and denied to the committee have been withheld on the pretext that they were interoffice memoranda, that they were working papers in the executive branch, and that therefore they were not final in the sense that they represented a final decision, and therefore Congress was not entitled to have such information.[3]

The resources available to the executive branch are so substantial that it has a capacity to amass, assess, and use

2. Op. cit., 161.
3. *Congressional Record*, 84th Cong., 2d sess., p. 11383.

information on almost any subject not equaled by any other province of the government. As Maryland Senator Charles McC. Mathias, Jr., said on July 28, 1971:

> The executive branch is, among other things, one of the more enormous information gathering machines ever devised by man. The Congress, on the other hand, in carrying out its unique responsibilities for assisting the President in the conduct of foreign policy must rely for information partly upon what it reads in the papers, partly upon whatever it can get from experts outside government, but most of all upon what the executive branch chooses to tell it.[4]

Implicit in this and similar comment is a view that the executive branch cannot be permitted to maintain its own surveillance, that it must reveal information to the Congress and generally to the public, and that there is no need for most of the secrecy involved. And as a practical matter, the Congress has no choice but to depend upon the executive branch for information since it is the primary and often the sole source for that information.

Senator Mathias put it this way:

> And if any President does not understand it, the Congress must insist upon it, must insist that if it is to carry out its constitutional responsibilities in foreign affairs, it must have access to the same information the President has—access to the documents, the recommendations, the advisers —especially those White House advisers whose influence upon foreign policy is far greater than that of any members of the Senate or even of the executive department.[5]

This position does not recognize that authority in foreign affairs is shared and the responsibilities of the president and the Congress are different. As Justice Sutherland

4. Senate, *Hearing*, 1971, p. 16.

5. Ibid., p. 17. Critics of the president's statement on executive privilege of March 12, 1973, called his claims "arrogant" and "executive poppycock," and charged it was designed to cover him from possible grave political embarrassment.

put it in *Belmont*, "governmental power over external affairs is not distributed, but is vested exclusively in the national government. And in respect of what was done here, the Executive had authority to speak as the sole organ of that government."[6] At issue was an executive agreement, and according to Sutherland, it did not require the advice and consent of the Senate to be binding.

By contrast, however, if the tenor of testimony is an accurate guide, was the comment during the 1971 hearing on executive privilege made by Senator Fulbright. "To state the matter in its simplest terms: if Congress does not investigate the Executive, there is no one to do it but the executive itself."[7]

Since the Congress is endowed with the power of inquiry and maintains that it has the duty of legislative oversight of government, the executive may properly be subject to inquiry on any subject and directed to any official of the executive branch, if Fulbright's position correctly reflects the view of the Congress. This denies to the executive branch any coequal status with the legislative, ignores any degree of independence for the executive, and if followed would put a practical end to the doctrine of separation of powers.

As Justice John M. Harlan said in *Barenblatt* v. *U.S.* in 1959:

> Broad as it is, the power is not, however, without limitations. Since Congress may only investigate into those areas in which it may potentially legislate or appropriate, it cannot inquire into matters which are within the exclusive province of one of the other branches of the Government. Lacking the judicial power given to the Judiciary, it cannot inquire into matters that are exclusively the concern of the Judiciary. Neither can it supplant the Executive in what exclusively belongs to the Executive.[8]

6. *U.S.* v. *Belmont*, 301 U.S. 324, 330 (1937).
7. Senate, *Hearing*, 1971, p. 25.
8. 360 U.S. 109, 122 (1959).

The primary congressional complaint against the executive branch in this respect is that information is denied and this denial is adverse to the concept of democracy. Justice Hugo Black wrote in 1941 that "freedom to speak and write about public questions is as important to the life of our government as is the heart of the human body. In fact, this privilege is the heart of our government. If that heart is weakened, the result is debilitation; if it be stilled, the result is death."[9]

Wigmore in *Evidence* wrote that "from the point of view of society's *right* to our testimony, it is to be remembered that the demand comes, not from any one person or set of persons, but from the community as a whole,—from justice as an institution, and from law and order as indispensable elements of civilized life."[10]

The ideal is for an enlightened choice by an informed citizenry, and it is certainly one upon which an open society is premised, and an incontestable precondition of self-government. One observer wrote more than fifty years ago:

> If a people are to be in a position to judge the conduct of their government, to decide whether it is doing well or ill, to decide the merits of public policy at all; if, indeed, they are to preserve the capacity for sound judgment, they must have facts before them not only as the government would have them put, but also as those who disagree with the government may desire to put them.[11]

But rights have limitations. The right to know is not unlimited. For purposes here, however, the issue is the extent to which that right is circumscribed by the "need to know."

9. *Milk Wagon Drivers' Union* v. *Meadowmoor Dairies*, 312 U.S. 287, 301, 302 (1941).

10. John Henry Wigmore, *A Treatise on the Anglo-American System of Evidence in Trials at Common Law*, 3d ed. (Boston: Little Brown & Co., 1940), 8:66.

11. Norman Angell, *The Press and the Organization of Society* (London: The Labour Publishing Co., 1922), p. 17.

The congressional quest for public policy, in and out of legislative halls, must include power adequate to acquire information and obtain testimony about legislative proposals and also about activities in which the government may be engaged. The congressional needs may be more extensive, however, than those of the public at large. At least the Congress sustains that position. It has done so not only through executive sessions of subcommittees and committees but also in legislation. These actions support the position that representatives of the body politic require some information which is not to be shared with the general citizenry.

The Congress has approved freedom-of-information legislation designed to permit easier access to information held by government agencies by anyone wanting it, but in so doing, has specified that some types of information could or should be controlled in whole or in part. It has further delineated the matter by providing that some types of information be given out under security classifications, thereby putting distinct qualifications on any right to know. Information can be withheld by the executive branch thereby not only from the general public, but also from the members of the Congress. It is public policy that some categories of information be controlled and it may be done either by statutory provisions in effect or additionally when the executive privilege is invoked. This distinction should be recognized to eliminate the confusion found in some writings when the two sources for information control are intertwined and presented as inseparable.

The search for public policy is a political act. The search and the policy product involve countless actors and influences. The route to a policy decision is usually not a simple one, and where a presumed popular will is not clear or a major division is apparent, the decision-making process may be a jumble of confusion and compromise.

Major public policy usually is a joint product, involving

the executive and the legislative branches. And since the product is a shared one, each of the partners, the president and the Congress, functions in their respective and somewhat separate spheres. Each responds frequently to problems and policy approaches from different settings, is affected by different forces and often with different objectives in view. Broad policy goals may not be in great dispute, but the elements which are a part of the composite result may well be.

The policymakers, the president and his advisers, members of the Congress who emerge as leaders, all have goals. These vary, as do the individuals who comprise the policymaking effort. Members of the House, coming as they do from single-member districts, have a wide range of positions on policy. What is of concern to one member may be of little or no concern to a member from another region, primarily because the interests of each constituency are so diverse. The attitudes and wants of a constituency have high priority with the House member, but these rarely come in a grand design for new policy.

Just as House members have distinct constituencies, so do their counterparts in the Senate. Furthermore, there are variables compounded by the great difference in the length of the terms of office. A House member, if he stays on, must continually mend his political fences. He must be alert continually to the political winds of his district, whatever his own views may be about any policy matter. A member of the Senate, on the other hand, may have a far more flexible position on issues and may not find it essential to have continual concern about his next election, at least for a time.

The sheer size of the House constricts the activity of individual members in the policymaking process. Members seek appointment or election to committees and subcommittees which they believe will provide the most service to their constituencies; or, taking what they can get, they hope to use the assignment as a steppingstone to another, preferred committee as their tenure is extended. The tendency in House operations is for a member to become a specialist in limited areas, and constituency influences may bear heavily in the decisions he makes.

A senator's state may give him many diverse interests to follow. But at the same time, he has a latitude in policy choices which may not be available to his House counterpart even from the same state. Senators presumably make a determination on the course of policy decision from fact, but also from judgments and notions of values. These become mixed and often confused and a final outcome may not square with fact or a rational decision. What is wanted may prevail, not what fact and rationale may suggest. Senators demonstrate they have opportunity and time in rendering judgments and opinions, outlining positions, and in engaging in the public spotlight in the club atmosphere of the Senate Chamber and sometimes more frequently when out of it.

Members of the Congress are political beings and the Congress itself is a political body. As such, political considerations guide their actions and are strong motivating factors in the course of any phase of legislative operations, especially in the course of inquiry. Spirited partisan differences are not infrequent and the varied individual characteristics of the members, often regardless of political party, may dominate the entire legislative process, including legislative oversight of administration. Political party cohesion is lacking as often as it prevails, perhaps more so, and on policy issues, the differences are substantial. Coalitions among conservatives and liberals, among Southern Democrats and conservative Republicans often provide the majorities rather than any strict party alignments.

Of especial interest in recent periods is the position frequently openly stated by the president prior to formal congressional vote. When confirmation voting in the Senate is taken, the president's position—which is obvious—may mean that more partisan coalitions will result than when no position is announced by the president. When, for example, the Senate considered the nomination of William P. Clements, Jr., as deputy secretary of defense on January 23, 1973, the Republican membership was solidly for approval, with the remainder of the votes needed coming from a mixture of Northern and Southern Democrats. Only one Southern Democrat opposed the nomination. In the 1973 debates about the irregularities in the 1972 presidential campaign, an attempt was made by some Senate Republicans to extend the inquiry into the 1964 and 1968 campaigns. No position was publicly announced by the president. The Republicans were nearly unanimous in support of it, but all Democrats opposed it, thereby defeating it. Whether a presidential position in favor would have altered the voting or the outcome is purely speculative.

The numerous subcommittees provide a ready forum for most members to pursue some form of inquiry. A senator of the majority party who chairs a subcommittee has a wide range of possible pursuits. Other subcommittee members, including those of the minority party, are similarly endowed with an opportunity to probe. The 1972–73 fiscal impoundment issues, for example, provided numerous senators from both parties excellent opportunities to engage in the kind of partisan political discourse which is common to the Congress of the United States.

Any examination of the hearings of subcommittees reveals the primary intent of the sponsors, but it also demonstrates the general lack of planning an inquiry. The kinds of queries by individual members show their diverse interests and motives. Furthermore, the increasing use of television in committee hearings has encouraged even the more timid to become political actors and to engage themselves more vigorously on occasion than they would have otherwise, in an earlier era.

These activities, however, are some of the essential

ingredients of the legislative function, even though only individual self-restraint prevents more of the often unmerciful "grilling" of executive branch officials by members of the Congress. The absence of a judicial setting which could ensure the propriety and pertinency of questions undoubtedly contributes to the spirited atmosphere which so often prevails.

Members of the Congress, especially those of the political party opposite to the president, who choose to lead inquiry into governmental operations naturally assume that there may be resistance to the inquiry from the executive branch. Since most programs of consequence are dominated by executive officials and even the president himself, it should be expected that these officials will present to the Congress, usually through the committee structure, that information which is intended to be favorable to the executive branch. Congressional opposition from opposite party adherents, or program opponents regardless of party, are thereby encouraged to seek out shortcomings, known or suspected, and attempt to elicit responses from often reluctant witnesses which may or may not be satisfying to the questioner. The results are often charges of lack of candor, unwillingness to admit to alleged shortcomings, bias, or favoritism in some form.

Most policy considerations are not completely new. They are restatements of existing policy, or may involve slight modifications, clarifications, or changes in emphasis or degrees of financial support. They evolve from long discussion, interest group consideration, hearings, and may involve planned or even unanticipated events. When a proposal is in the category of being new, its source is likely not the Congress, but the president.

In the policymaking sphere, the president is usually the most influential and prestigious. Only a few in the Congress can match the political power available to a president. When the president speaks, the nation will hear him whether they listen or not. His position, his views, his arguments, his persuasion, his choice of timing, all bear heavily on policy outcomes. And as presidents have come and gone, as individuals they have shaped the presidency for their successors in some way. This heritage is there and ready for a successor's use. A president is also endowed with a more nearly national constituency than any member of the Congress and he knows it. He can oppose that which is dear to a member of the House and have no great distress. He can promote that which is opposed by many members and succeed in it.

In the course of policy determination a possible confrontation between Congress and the president may result from the problem of who should determine what information the executive branch should give out so that the Congress can legislate wisely and in the public interest. As Representative E. E. Cox of Georgia observed at one time, "Where rests the power to determine what the public interest is? . . . Is Congress to be rendered powerless to determine for itself what is or is not in the public interest? If this be so, then who is to legislate in the public interest—or is there to be no legislation at all?"[12]

The historical arguments favoring the power of the Congress to obtain information it wants generally rest on the statement found in resolutions that agencies make available "to any and all standing, special, or select committees of the House of Representatives and the Senate," information "which may be deemed necessary to enable them to properly perform the duties delegated to them by the Congress."

Much of the Congress's direction to the executive branch is to the departments and agencies which the Congress created. If the Congress has the power to create or not create, then can it not determine how these agencies function? Since it is also charged with the power to provide

12. *Congressional Record*, 78th Cong., 2d sess., p. 1034.

or not provide funds, then in the fulfillment of that authority, it should be able to obtain information it desires. "Shall the Congress insist that departments created by it, dependent upon its will for existence, give to its committees the information necessary to enable it to act intelligently and wisely, or shall it permit its creatures to arbitrarily determine what information the Congress shall or shall not have?"[13]

A different facet of this issue of executive control of information arises when the judicial branch is involved. In litigation in the courts, a difference is drawn between information which an individual may request for his own benefit in either a criminal or civil suit or trial and information which a committee of the Congress may want. Requests of the former kind are frequent, and most of them appear to have been disposed of without difficulty and to the satisfaction of the litigants and the agencies of the government involved. These range widely from information from a regulatory agency or even a cabinet department. At issue, usually, is whether the release of information in a trial would be prejudicial or contrary to the public interest. Statutes and executive orders and directives have guided both the release and the restrictions. Reports involving business activities submitted to a government agency in confidence which, if released, might adversely affect that business have been subject to withholding by court determination. Papers involving the internal workings of a department have been withheld with success. Files concerning employment records of individuals also may be protected from requested disclosure.

These activities and inquiries ordinarily involve subordinate executive branch activity even though the claim of "privilege" may be made. It is a claim that what is wanted is privileged information and not that the president has

13. U.S. Congress, House of Representatives, *Report No. 1595*, pt. 1, 80th Cong., 2d sess., p. 4.

authorized or directed invoking the executive privilege. These lower-echelon claims provide both interest and controversy and are often reported as claims of *executive* privilege even when they have not had any direct presidential involvement.[14]

In times of domestic distress a president likely has the upper hand in his role as political leader and molder of public opinion. He may have it also at many other times, but in the realm of external affairs or domestic matters which bear directly on the course of external affairs it is the president who commands. But it is in the search for policy and policy direction in external affairs that much dispute has developed over the sharing of power between the legislative and executive branches. Presenting and maintaining one voice or position on a complex of external matters and having differences of consequence stop at the water's edge are as rare as they are frequent. A president can have the dominant, if not exclusive, position through his control over foreign operations even though he may not wholly determine that position.

In the dispute between President Nixon and the Senate Foreign Relations Committee in 1971 over foreign aid, the subject of the dispute was as much the substance of foreign aid as it was the policymaking process and the availability of information about other nations' wants or needs, but these were overshadowed by a claim of the fiscal capacity of the United States to support it. Foreign military

14. Illustrative is the 1973 report that the secretary of the Air Force "invoked executive privilege" in refusing to answer questions about some airplane cost overruns before a civil service examiner. He did so, he said, because he had received some advice on the matter from the White House. He did not say the advice was from the president. It must be remembered, however, that Chief Justice John Marshall said of the president in *Marbury* v. *Madison*, 1 Cr. 137, 166 (1802), that "to aid him in the performance of these duties [the president's] he is authorized to appoint certain officers, who act by his authority, and in conformity with his orders. *In such cases, their acts are his acts*." Emphasis supplied. This is considered in Chapter V.

assistance and foreign economic aid have been continued from inception under the Truman Doctrine and the Marshall Plan at the insistence of every president since Truman. Foreign aid of whatever variety or extent, however, has no ready-made constituency in the United States, at least not a very strong one. Authorizations for assistance and appropriations have been under challenge continually. Efforts to reduce aid substantially or even eliminate it have had strong support at each legislative session. Faced with this opposition, the executive branch has found it necessary to alter the emphasis, the amounts, the objectives and even change the name of the administering agency in order to present a plan viable enough to satisfy members of the Congress who would support the aid and get its continuation.

President Truman presented the foreign aid program with emphasis on humanitarian considerations.[15] But searching questions have been asked ever since. Is foreign aid an attempt to help the poor countries—more recently called the developing countries—in their goals toward

15. In his fourth point, Truman stated:

> We must embark on a bold new program for making the benefits of our scientific advances and individual progress available for the improvement and growth of underdeveloped areas.
>
> More than half the people of the world are living in conditions approaching misery. Their food is inadequate. They are victims of disease. Their economic life is primitive and stagnant. Their poverty is a handicap and a threat both to them and to more prosperous areas.
>
> For the first time in history humanity possesses the knowledge and the skill to relieve the suffering of these people.
>
> The United States is preeminent among nations in the development of industrial and scientific techniques. The material resources which we can afford to use for the assistance of other peoples are limited. But our imponderable resources in technical knowledge are constantly growing and are inexhaustible.
>
> I believe that we should make available to peace-loving peoples the benefits of our store of technical knowledge in order to help them realize their aspirations for a better life.

economic development? This is a laudable position and one which, if successful, would hopefully put the leadership of the recipient nations on the side of the United States in the international realm. Or, was the real purpose of the aid, military and economic, to promote the security of the United States? If the latter, was the security of the United States to be maintained and extended only if the aid programs stemmed the march of Communism? The Truman Doctrine was a policy for containment of Communism, and the machinery to make it effective was foreign aid. Congresses responded and have continued to respond favorably, but not without voicing strong reservations about its successes and the emphasis given it. Many voices have long been heard that this program is not even a veiled attempt to buy foreign support for the overseas policies of the United States.

There has not been prospect that foreign aid would suddenly end. As recently as October 11, 1973, when the Congress failed to pass the annual appropriation bill for military aid, interim support was provided.[16]

The vast array of proposals for legislation which involve changes in existing statutes always gives the Congress ample opportunity to review the "execution of the laws" and to make changes as it sees fit. How many of these proposals have their beginnings in hearings or in the executive agencies involved or with members of the Congress or committee staffs is not easily determined, but it is in the initiation of legislation that the Congress can and should play its most important role. Whatever course of oversight the Congress gives administration, it has continu-

16. *Congressional Record*, 92d Cong., 2d sess., p. D1153. Senator Fulbright said at the time that the Agency for International Development was undertaking to "build a constituency" for foreign aid through announcements of the amounts being spent in the several states for equipment and supplies of various kinds.

ous opportunity to alter its delegations for administrative action.

A major criticism of the Congress is that it needs to overhaul its methods if it is to respond to the demands of the future and that it cannot ply its old ways. One change is to alter the slogan that "the president proposes and the Congress disposes." To reverse it somewhat would mean a greater input from the Congress in the initiation of legislation. How far this would go in tempering the conflicts about the executive domination is not known, but it could mean a reassertion of position in the legislative role of the Congress.

Activist presidents are not hesitant in proposing legislation. Nor has the Congress been as hesitant as critical commentary suggests. Any student of the legislative process knows how complicated the enactment of laws may be. What is wanted? How are problems identified and solutions found? What different methods of solving problems can be discovered? How can the best or most appropriate alternative be selected and agreed to? Which will be most acceptable to those elements of society which may be affected?

Whatever the rightness of criticisms about seniority on congressional committees, some expertise is gained from extended service on a committee. This specialization renders the Congress into splinter groupings, but to operate otherwise could mean that the Congress would be almost wholly dependent upon staff work or even more upon the executive branch. The members of the Congress do not operate in a closed environment. They and their staffs are constantly in communication with their often diverse constituencies. This is especially true for members of the House. They gain much from these associations, which form the source of much legislation that may be said to be inititated within the Congress. The major problem, however, is not that proposals cannot be initiated and find their way into the congressional "hopper," but one of finding agreement to form a majority action.

In this process does the Congress obtain necessary information to fulfill its legislative function? That is the issue about the exercise of the executive privilege. But it is also common knowledge that with whatever information the Congress has available to it, it has difficulty making a decision. Although when measures from the Congress are presented for consideration to the president he does not have much time for decision, he is or may be as well informed throughout the entire legislative process as any member of the Congress.

But the legislative process is not as simple as that. There is continuous liaison between the bureaucracy and members of the Congress and the committee staffs. One evidence of this liaison is that there may be continuous interchange as the legislative process goes on and no doubt there is "smuggling" from one to the other in the search for mutual support.[17] These are some of the ways, by design, to provide executive counterproposals, which may be called the "president's bills."

The clamor about usurpation of legislative powers in 1965 was given this response by Representative Moss when he said that the Congress can "use its own rights and privileges in seeking to get its information."[18] The Congress is not as helpless as some of its members would have the public believe.

Section 3 of Article II of the U.S. Constitution provides that the president "shall from time to time give to the Congress information of the State of the Union, and recommend to their Consideration such Measures as he shall

17. John R. Johannes, "Congress and the Initiation of Legislation," *Public Policy*, Spring 1972, p. 289.

18. U.S. Congress, House of Representatives, *Hearings before a Subcommittee of the House Committee on Government Operations: "Federal Public Records Law,"* 89th Cong., 1st sess., 1965, p. 23.

judge necessary and expedient."[19] Presidents have used this grant of authority to choose those matters which they and their advisers consider the most appropriate at a given time. With the advent of radio and, later, television, the forum for the presentation of information has vastly broadened from presentations to the Congress and some newspaper coverage to being viewed and heard by countless millions of people at home and abroad. In this way, a president can select topics for especial emphasis and it is at his discretion to choose some and ignore others. He can cause topics to have national focus and his recommendations become the front runners for any policymaking.

The flexibility available to a president in framing his policy choices may be far greater than for the Congress. A president can present a single course of action, setting forth his plans in legislative format. A new president may be delayed in so doing and for proper reason. This was highlighted during the first months of 1969 when House Speaker John W. McCormack of Massachusetts replied to critics about the slow pace of the Congress by saying that the House, at least, was waiting for the president to send up his bills.

A president can select his programs with some latitude and discretion. In foreign affairs, for example, his choices may be based upon recommendations from ambassadors or other advisers. Diplomats need to be on favorable terms with officials of the country to which they are accredited and may recommend a proposal because it is a good political choice. Whether the choice becomes a part of United States policy is a choice ultimately for the United States, but presidents know that if benefits are to come to the United States from it, some consideration may have to be

19. It has been claimed that this is a requirement that a president fully inform the Congress even at the direction of the Congress. But that is a tortured interpretation of this constitutional provision where *his* judgment is involved and judgment is a discretionary act.

given even to choices for only tactical political purposes.

The extent to which this kind of information needs to be distributed for the Congress to be properly informed has been the source of some debate over the need of the Congress to know. The Constitution gives the president authority over the negotiating aspects of any agreements with other nations, and this he need not share with the Congress. His discussions with foreign representatives are clearly in the executive realm and need not be shared. But when funds are required or agreements are to be ratified as treaties, then the Congress properly enters the scene. In making a decision, information must be provided and the major source is the executive branch. Clearly, the Congress cannot be denied essential information or it would be merely a "rubber stamp" for the executive branch. The focus by the Congress, however, should be on recommendations presented and not the process by which they may have been produced.

During the 1957 debate over the Mutual Security Act, Senator Theodore F. Green of Rhode Island said that the Foreign Relations and the Appropriations Committees of the Senate "have always been able to get all the information they need about mutual-security programs."[20] But what is needed and what is adequate are not matters upon which all members of the Congress might agree.

Although presidents have exercised the executive privilege or extended it in some manner to restrict disclosures by subordinates for a variety of reasons, the privilege must rest on some constitutional grounds or it would exist only, if at all, upon congressional prescription and consent. If, as maintained here, it has a constitutional basis, then the president's primacy in foreign relations, national defense, and security makes it essential that the executive branch follow the admonition by Senator Fulbright that "one branch must, occasionally, accord to the

20. *Congressional Record*, 85th Cong., 1st sess., p. 9151.

other branch a certain degree of trust" and make documents and testimony available on some basis.[21] There is no indication that the Congress possesses information needed or wanted by the president.

Opponents of the executive privilege as having a constitutional basis generally do not examine carefully the grants of power to the executive and legislative branches. Article II vests the *executive power* in *a* president. Article I states that "all legislative powers herein granted shall be vested in a Congress of the United States." The words "herein granted" are not contained in the Executive Article and give support to executive power beyond the few explicit powers stated in that article.

The Steel Seizure Case sheds some light.[22] Only one justice clearly stated that the president had general executive powers. Four others joined him in rejecting the Truman claim in this particular case since the Congress had made provisions by statute governing strikes. In the absence of any legislation would the outcome have been different? The decision does not indicate that the constitutional grant of executive power is limited to the specifics of the Executive Article or that executive powers must rest on congressional authority. Such a reading would reduce the presidency to an almost ceremonial status.

The executive privilege is usually challenged because it means some degree of secrecy. But since Washington's time the need for secrecy in dealing with other nations has been recognized. It may be argued further that secret diplomacy may also be the best diplomacy. Whether true or not, secrecy in foreign affairs and also in national

21. Ibid., p. 9150.

22. *Youngstown Sheet & Tube* v. *Sawyer*, op. cit. Three justices agreed with the president. The decision, however, does not appear to support the position that the constitutional grant of power to the executive is limited to the specifics which follow the general grant of power. Such a reading would reduce the executive power to a general first-class clerkship.

defense gives a president not only a substantial advantage, but severely restricts any serious competition from anyone else. A president can obtain vast amounts of information because of his authority in these areas, and because of his ability to get it he dominates his rivals in the Congress or elsewhere. Not only can he generally succeed because of superior resources, but his chances for success are enhanced with usually weak, divided opposition or because the opposition does not have strong beliefs it should control foreign policy.[23]

But some of the rivals are strongly persistent. On July 29, 1971, the Senate Committee on Foreign Relations voted, without dissent, to invoke a provision in the 1961 Foreign Assistance Act that spending for a foreign aid activity would be suspended if within thirty-five days the executive branch had not supplied a document requested by a congressional committee or the General Accounting Office. The issue involved the five-year projections for country aid which were not supplied at the time. The funds cutoff would not take place, however, if the president would personally forbid the release of the requested documents and gave a reason.[24] Later, however, Secretary of State Rogers announced that some information on proposed country assistance would be given to the committee. He said, "I think . . . we can comply with your request. I think it is reasonable."[25] This conflict, like others about restricting information requested by the Congress, is an indication that the president or his chief subordinates believed the members of the committee should not be

23. President Nixon's approaches to the People's Republic of China in 1972 are illustrative.

24. David M. Abshire, assistant secretary of state for congressional relations, Department of State, said later that in the field of foreign affairs the president had refused to supply information on only two occasions. One was on military assistance planning, the other involved internal working papers about the U.S. Information Agency.

25. *New York Times*, September 9, 1971.

taken into confidence or that the confidence would probably be violated. A disclosure might or might not damage the security of the United States, but it might damage the security of other nations involved or violate their own policies about such disclosure. Candor in such matters is laudable if only our government is involved, but in external matters others are also involved.

The executive branch's position on United States propaganda abroad came under attack early in 1972 when Senator Fulbright stated that unless planning documents involving the U.S. Information Agency's overseas activities were made available to his committee, funds for the agency might be blocked. The staff of the Foreign Relations Committee had asked the agency to supply it with program memoranda and planning papers which were used in preparing the budget request, stating they were needed in order to pass judgment on the request. The agency director stated that the documents were "unevaluated" and were working papers from officers in various countries and did not represent official agency policy. He insisted that if they were made public "it would stifle everybody" and "all you would get from the field would be mush."[26]

Unevaluated working papers might have been interesting reading, but would they have served appropriately or qualified in rendering judgment for funds? The issue with the committee was the type of programming being done by the agency. Senator Fulbright charged that the agency was undermining the president's policy of negotiation and following a policy of confrontation with Communist nations. He gave one example to support his contention. The agency's policy directive for Colombia stated that a

26. Ibid., March 21, 1972. Charles D. Ablard, general counsel, USIA, testified on March 15, 1972, that "to the best of my knowledge, this was the first time that the Agency materials had been denied to a congressional committee." See House, *Hearings . . . on Government Operations*, 1972, p. 3237.

major objective of its program should be to "alert Colombians to the dangers of Communist solutions of national problems."[27]

The Senate shares with the president the appointment of members of the cabinet, among others. In considering the 1972 nomination of Richard Kleindienst as attorney general, the Senate Committee on the Judiciary became involved in an inquiry about an antitrust settlement by the Department of Justice for the International Telephone and Telegraph Company. It was charged that some improper influence had been used in the case, and not being satisfied with the information it had received, the committee directed a request that presidential aide Peter M. Flanigan testify about the case. The invitation was refused but an accommodation was reached so that he agreed to give some testimony. He wrote the committee on April 18, 1972, as follows:

> Dear Mr. Chairman:
>
> On April 10, 1972, Mr. John Dean, Counsel to the President, responded to your Committee's invitation to me to appear and testify in connection with the Committee's hearing relating to the confirmation of Mr. Richard Kleindienst as Attorney General. Mr. Dean's letter explained that I could not accept an invitation calling for testimony relating to the performance of my duties as a member of the immediate staff of the President.
>
> Since that time, several members of the Judiciary Committee have indicated that the testimony sought from me relates solely to my limited involvement in assisting former Assistant Attorney General McLaren in obtaining independent financial analysis and Mr. Geneen's participation in a group meeting in February, 1971.
>
> If the Committee feels that my testimony in respect to the foregoing would be of assistance in its consideration of Mr. Kleindienst's confirmation and the scope of my appear-

27. *New York Times*, March 21, 1972.

ance is limited accordingly, I would welcome the opportunity to appear and testify before your Committee.

I respectfully await the Committee's decision.

Sincerely yours,
Peter M. Flanigan,
Assistant to the President.[28]

This compromise with the committee is indicative of the kind of accord which can be reached with the Congress in the exercise of its powers.[29]

The Amchitka nuclear tests, considered above, involved a mixture of some aspects of executive privilege and congressional control over information held by the executive branch.[30] The circumstances are reflected in an affidavit.

On June 27, 1969, the President directed the Under Sec-

28. U.S. Congress, Senate, *Hearings before the Committee on the Judiciary*, pt. 3, *Nomination of Richard G. Kleindienst, of Arizona, to Be Attorney General*, 92d Cong., 2d sess., 1972, p. 1413.

29. The resolution by the Committee on the Judiciary of April 18, 1972, contained the following:

> The Committee agrees to hear the testimony of Peter M. Flanigan upon the conditions set out in Mr. Flanigan's letter of April 18, 1972, with the understanding that its members may interrogate him upon the following matters:
>
> 1. His knowledge in respect to the selection of San Diego as the site of the Republican National Convention;
>
> 2. The matters which occurred in his presence at the meetings held in the office of Attorney General on April 29, 1971.
>
> The Committee understands that Mr. Flanigan is not required to testify to any knowledge based on confidential communications between him and the President or between him and other aides of the President.
>
> All questions by whomever asked shall be treated by the witness as so limited, and the witness will not be required to state any reason for not answering any question that the Chair rules to be not germane. [Ibid., p. 1630]

Senator Edward M. Kennedy said that he would not be bound completely by the conditions set forth in the resolution.

30. See the Freedom of Information Act, 5. U.S.C., sec. 552.

> retaries Committee to review the annual underground nuclear test program and to encompass within this review requests for authorization of specific scheduled tests. He directed that the Committee consider the policy and technical justification for the proposed tests to determine whether they are consistent with the requirements of national security and foreign policy. He requested that the results of the Committee's review of the underground nuclear tests programs and its recommendations be transmitted to him in time to allow him to give them full consideration before the scheduled events.[31]

Some of the reports were given security classifications and it was claimed that the "information in the documents described . . . which is not public necessarily is held in strict confidence by the Government in order to prevent grave damage to our national defense and foreign policy interests."[32]

Prior to presidential approval of the tests, efforts were made in the House of Representatives to prevent them from being conducted at all. One was to deny funds to carry out the tests. A second and also unsuccessful attempt was made when a Senate-House conference on fund denial was rejected by a House vote.[33]

When reports were circulated that the president's approval of the tests was based on conflicting recommendations, the action was instituted by members of the House to compel disclosure of some of the documents in the reports which ultimately reached the U.S. Supreme Court in *Environmental Protection Agency v. Mink*.[34] The U.S. district court held in favor of executive determination of dis-

31. The solicitor general's brief in *Environmental Protection Agency* v. *Mink*, op. cit., p. 4.

32. Ibid., p. 7.

33. *Congressional Record*, 92d Cong., 1st sess., p. 25228.

34. The action was instituted by thirty-three members of the House acting in a private capacity. See *Mink* v. *Environmental Protection Agency*, op. cit.

closure, but the court of appeals reversed. The Supreme Court agreed to consider the issue on March 6, 1972, and gave its decision on January 22, 1973. As already indicated, the government did not claim executive privilege and relied wholly on the applicable statute. What is of significance, however, is the statement in the majority opinion that the Congress could adopt different procedures if it wished, but "—subject only to whatever limitations the Executive privilege may be held to impose upon such congressional ordering."[35]

Although in this case a statute was at issue, the decision has many implications for the executive privilege. In his concurring opinion, Justice Potter Stewart said the case presented no constitutional claims and no issues regarding the nature or scope of executive privilege.[36] The two opinions, both mentioning executive privilege, do not answer the question whether there is a constitutional basis for the privilege since it was not claimed by the government.[37]

One unanswered question about the "need to know" is whether it was intended by the framers of the Constitution that there be two constitutional standards in controlling information, one for the Congress and another for the other two branches. The Constitution is specific in granting secrecy to the Congress. It is silent for the other branches. Was this an intentional difference? If so, then the executive and judicial branches possess no constitutional authority to withhold information, or when they do, they have only such authority as the Congress may grant to them. The judicial branch fully asserts and exercises information control and it is respected by the legislative

35. This may be the first time the court has used a capital *E* in a decision involving the executive privilege.

36. The statute involved and the court's decision are evidences of attempts to police the privilege and will be considered in a later chapter.

37. No claim of executive privilege was made in *Soucie* v. *David*, op. cit.

branch. If the three branches are in fact coequals, then the Congress must respect the executive privilege.[38]

In the course of events and the contests over the exercise of the executive privilege the Congress has not fared badly in the outcome and in getting the information it wanted. Some of the more insatiable appetites have not been satisfied and efforts continue to brake and police the privilege.

It remains a matter of opinion whether the exercise of executive privilege is any real limitation on information required by the Congress in fulfilling its constitutional responsibilities. When it is, it may be that it is more important to preserve a balance between the legislative and executive branches than to have the legislative branch dominate the executive branch. With recent issues about respecting the confidence between the president and his aides, the contest between the president and the Congress may reach a point where the U.S. Supreme Court may be faced with meeting the issue squarely. If it does, it will have to consider positions not unlike the 1972 suggestion that salaries be denied officials who refuse to testify before congressional committees. Representative William S. Moorhead of Pennsylvania observed:

> A witness such as Dr. Kissinger does not personally have an executive privilege. It is only the President who enjoys and can invoke this privilege. It may be concluded from this that the salary cut-off is intended to apply to situations in which a government official is prohibited from testifying on the basis of the President's assertion of the doctrine of executive privilege. So interpreted, the legislation is of doubtful constitutionality. . . .
>
> Executive privilege is one of the well-recognized limitations on the power of Congress to investigate. The doctrine is rooted on the ground of separation of powers. . . . Thus,

38. Senator Sam J. Ervin, Jr., of North Carolina has responded to similar statements, saying "I recognize the validity of executive privilege when it is limited to its proper scope."

> Congress cannot directly compel the testimony of a person for whom the President invokes executive privilege.[39]

The relationships between the executive and legislative branches often demonstrate the heavy dependence the Congress has upon the executive agencies, including the president, in carrying out its tasks of legislation and inquiry. Furthermore, the relationships show distinct elements of bargaining between them. The results on a given issue or series of related issues are usually in the form of some compromise, with neither branch being wholly successful nor necessarily satisfied with the results.

Members of the Congress and the president and his subordinates compete in the total political process and this competition is a consequence of the tripartite arrangement for government. Frictions which result may be settled through compromise, or later at the ballot box, or by the forces of public opinion or even in the courts. The process usually, however, involves some balancing of interests.

In these interchanges, control over information may be in the center of issues. But the control is primarily, if not almost wholly, a matter of executive control, since it is the Congress which seeks information from the executive branch and *not* the converse.

A president, however, strives usually to improve his position and not to reduce it. In exercising his discretionary control over information he is able to modify his stand and arrive at some acceptable conclusion. Indeed, the results may be the goal desired or anticipated by both the Congress and the president. The objective in reaching agreement is not necessarily information control for the sake of secrecy, but the expectation of some gains at the bargaining table.

39. *Congressional Record*, 92d Cong., 2d sess., p. H6006.

V

Executive Privacy

At the time of the trial in Chicago, Illinois, in November, 1969, of the "Chicago Seven" involving those individuals alleged to have conspired to incite riots during the 1968 National Democratic Convention, a member of the legal staff defending the seven men announced that subpoenas were being drawn to obtain appearances and testimony from Senators Eugene J. McCarthy and J. William Fulbright, former attorney general Ramsey Clark, and former president Lyndon B. Johnson.[1]

If a subpoena had been issued and served on the former president, it is likely that he would have chosen to refuse to honor it if it were designed to cause him to testify about matters involving his tenure as president. But that circumstance did not take place. The subpoena was not issued.

The proposition that an effort would have been made to question the former president in a judicial setting is of significance since it raises the question whether there is a right to executive privacy, a right to official silence by a president even after he leaves that office, if he is asked to testify about matters affecting his office. The more basic question, however, is whether any claim to privacy is constitutionally protected when a president or

1. *Lincoln Evening Journal*, November 11, 1969.

former president is presented with a judicial or legislative directive to answer questions about his performance while in office.[2] President Truman's statement, cited above, was a categorical denial of any right of anyone to force a president to be called to account for his official actions or his knowledge about them.

In *State of Mississippi* v. *Johnson*, decided in 1867, the U.S. Supreme Court said that the president was put beyond the reach of judicial direction in the exercise of any of his powers, whether constitutional or statutory, political or otherwise.[3]

The Constitution is silent on the subject of executive privacy. As has been noted, secrecy is specifically authorized for the Congress, but not for the other branches. In the absence of a provision for executive or judicial privacy each of these branches has sought to prevent intrusions into its respective counsels regardless of any constitutional authority. The Congress has recognized elements of privacy for the executive branch from time to time and, as illustrated by the Freedom of Information Act, authorized broad categories of information which could be exempt from scrutiny. But these are statutory prescriptions and are subject to change.

When President Eisenhower signed an act in 1959 containing a provision designed to force the executive branch to submit any and all information considered by the Congress as "necessary in the evaluation of the foreign aid program," he issued the following statement:

> I have signed this bill on the express premise that the three amendments relating to the disclosure are not intended to alter and cannot alter the recognized Constitutional duty and power of the Executive with respect to the disclosure of information, documents and other materials. Indeed, any other construction of these amendments would

2. If a president cannot be compelled to respond, it does not mean that his acts cannot be made subject to inquiry and review.

3. 4 Wall. 475.

raise grave Constitutional questions under the Separation of Powers Doctrine.[4]

Presumably this advice was given to the president by then Attorney General Rogers. Rogers had stated in his 1957 reply to Senator Hennings that "communications between the President and the Attorney General are confidential and not subject to inquiry by a committee of one of the Houses of Congress."[5]

John Marshall sought to distinguish between documents which a president could control and those which might be public. He said at the time of the Burr trial that "letters to the President in his private character, are often written to him in consequence of his public character, and may relate to a public concern. Such a letter though it be a private one, seems to partake of an official paper, and ought not on light ground to be forced into public view."[6]

Years later President Cleveland indicated that there was executive privacy associated with the executive power. In his message of March 1, 1866, he reasoned that those papers in executive departments, including his own office, which were purely executive in nature, or which were private in nature, remained subject to the control of the executive, whereas those involving matters in which the Congress had a right to participate were proper for disclosure. Tyler's refusal, noted above, was based on a claim that release would prejudice a prosecution and do harm to individuals and also would not be in the public interest. The Tyler action was a reiteration of the position taken much earlier by Jefferson when he denied the House of Representatives access to papers involving an executive inquiry into an alleged criminal conspiracy. Cleveland's position was that there was no implied or actual "lien" in

4. *Public Papers: Eisenhower*, p. 549.
5. Rogers, "Memorandums," 1958, p. 23.
6. Quoted in Rogers, "Memorandums," 1958, p. 36.

favor of the Congress over the executive departments even though the latter had been created by statute. He refused to give public character to papers and documents solely because they were *in* executive departments. "There is no mysterious power of transmutation in department custody, nor is there magic in the undefined and sacred solemnity of Department files."[7]

How is a distinction to be made between the papers which are of an executive nature and those which are of proper legislative concern? And who makes the decision? Cleveland obviously considered this to be an executive act, for otherwise, the executive, meaning the president, would be subject to detailed surveillance by the Congress.

If Cleveland's position is given its full impact, then a president exercises complete control for all time over papers held by him or he could completely destroy them. The extent of this use of executive privacy involving papers was later described by President Theodore Roosevelt. "Some of these facts which they want, for what purpose I hardly know, were given to the Government under the seal of secrecy and cannot be divulged, and I will see to it that the word of this Government to the individual is kept sacred."[8] Not only could the executive refuse to permit disclosure, he could personally command possession of papers and fully control them until such time as he saw fit to release them.

If there is a constitutional basis for executive privacy, it must rest on the doctrine of the separation of powers. If this privacy is inherent in the executive power of the president as stated in the Constitution, then there is a formidable claim to the exercise of executive privilege in the control a president has over papers in the executive branch.[9] The claim can also be extended to control testimony.

7. Richardson, *Messages and Papers of the Presidents*, 8:378.
8. Abbott, *Letters of Archibald Butt*, p. 306.
9. When extended to subordinates the control may not be complete,

In *Marbury* v. *Madison*, Chief Justice John Marshall indicated there was some form of privacy within the president's official family.

> By the Constitution of the United States, the president is invested with certain political powers, in the exercise of which he is to use his own discretion, and is accountable only to his country in his political character, and to his conscience. To aid him in the performance of these duties, he is authorized to appoint certain officers, who act by his authority, and in conformity with his orders. In such cases, their acts are his acts; and whatever opinion may be entertained of the manner in which executive discretion may be used, still there exists, and can exist, no power to control that discretion.[10]

Years later, in *Myers* v. *U.S.*, Chief Justice William Howard Taft considered the element of presidential discretion, stating that

> the discretion to be exercised is that of the President in determining the national public interest and in directing the action to be taken by his executive subordinates to protect it. In this field his cabinet officers must do his will. He must place in each member of his official family, and his chief executive subordinates, implicit faith. The moment he loses confidence in the intelligence, ability, judgment or loyalty of any one of them, he must have the power to remove him without delay. To require him to file charges and submit them to the consideration of the Senate might make impossible that unity and co-ordination in executive administration essential to effective action.[11]

The chief justice emphasized confidence and confi-

---

but it is strong enough to be a resisting force notwithstanding threats of subpoenas. The Senate Committee on the Judiciary on April 12, 1972, for example, refused to issue a subpoena to compel testimony from presidential aides.

10. Op. cit., 165.
11. Op. cit.

dence denotes that communications made in confidence not be subject to demands for external release.[12]

Professor E. S. Corwin summarized the issue whether a president could maintain confidences and deny them from inquiry in this way.

> In short, no one questions, or can question, the constitutional right of the houses to inform themselves through committees of inquiry on subjects that fall within their legislative competence and to hold in contempt recalcitrant witnesses before such committees, and undoubtedly the question of employee loyalty is such a subject. On the other hand, this prerogative of Congress has always been regarded as limited by the right of the President to have his subordinates refuse to testify either in court or before a committee of Congress *concerning matters of confidence between them and himself.*[13]

In his concurring opinion in *New York Times* v. *U.S.*, Justice Potter Stewart gave support to executive privacy in this manner. "It is clear to me that it is the constitutional duty of the Executive—as a matter of sovereign prerogative and not as a matter of law as the courts know law—through the promulgation and enforcement of executive regulations, to protect the confidentiality necessary to carry out its responsibilities in the fields of international relations and national defense."[14]

12. Presidential assistants in recent decades originated from the recommendation by the President's Committee on Administrative Management in 1937. "They would remain in the background, issue no orders, make no decisions," and would be "men in whom the President has personal confidence and whose character and attitude is such that they would not attempt to exercise power on their own account" (*Report of the Committee* [Washington, D.C.: U.S. Government Printing Office, 1937], p. 5). A later analysis described presidential assistants as "an extension of the Presidency itself" (Barry Dean Karl, *Executive Reorganization and Reform in the New Deal* [Cambridge: Harvard University Press, 1963], p. 241).

13. Edward S. Corwin, *The President: Office and Powers*, 4th ed. (New York: New York University Press, 1957), p. 116. Emphasis supplied.

14. Op. cit., 729, 730.

In his dissenting opinion, Chief Justice Warren Berger, in a footnote, made this observation:

> With respect to the question of inherent power of the Executive to classify papers, records and documents as secret, or otherwise unavailable for public exposure, and to secure aid of the courts for enforcement, there may be an analogy with respect to this Court. No statute gives this Court express power to establish the utmost security measures for the secrecy of our deliberations and records. Yet I have little doubt as to the inherent power of the Court to protect the confidentiality of its internal operations by whatever judicial measures may be required.[15]

These two statements provide strong support for executive privacy. Justice Stewart wrote of the confidentiality necessary in international relations and national defense and not confidentiality in general. Whether this was because the issues there involved only those matters is not clear, but the language appears adequate to extend confidentiality further.

Earlier, in 1948, executive privacy in foreign affairs was considered by Justice Robert H. Jackson in *Chicago & Southern Air Lines* v. *Waterman Steamship Corp.*

> The very nature of executive decisions as to foreign policy is political, not judicial. Such decisions are wholly confided by our Constitution to the political departments of the government, Executive and Legislative. They are delicate, complex, and involve large elements of prophecy. They are and should be undertaken only by those directly responsible to the people whose welfare they advance or imperil.[16]

Foreign policy is a shared power, but the president has

15. Ibid., 752.

16. Op. cit., 103, 111. The majority opinion in *Environmental Protection Agency* v. *Mink* op. cit., does not support Jackson. "The burden is, of course, on the agency resisting disclosure . . . and if it fails to meet its burden without *in camera* inspection, the District Court may order such inspection."

primacy in negotiations. As John Marshall said when a member of the House of Representatives in 1800, "the President is the sole organ of the nation in its external relations, and its sole representative with foreign nations."[17]

During the 1951 inquiry into the military situation in the Far East by the Senate Committee on Armed Forces and the Committee on Foreign Relations, General Omar N. Bradley, then chairman of the Joint Chiefs of Staff, was testifying in response to questions about the president's removal of General Douglas MacArthur from his Far East command assignment. The record shows the following:

Meeting with the President, April 6, 1951

The first time I really came into this, and found out what it was all about, was on Friday morning, April 6, when I met with the President, and the others in his office, at which time he explained what his concern was.

SENATOR WILEY. All right, now; we are coming to April 6, the one you just mentioned, Friday morning.

You said at that time there was the President; there was the Joint Chiefs of Staff—

GENERAL BRADLEY. No, sir; I did not say the Joint Chiefs.

SENATOR WILEY. I beg your pardon.

You said there was Marshall, Acheson—and who else?

GENERAL BRADLEY. Harriman and myself.

Relationship of Advisers to the President

SENATOR WILEY. All right.

No, tell us what was said then.

GENERAL BRADLEY. Senator, at that time I was in a position of a confidential adviser to the President. I do not feel at liberty to publicize what any of us said at that time.

SENATOR WILEY. Well, that raises a question, I suppose, that the Chair will have to rule on.

I didn't raise it with Marshall, because I was in a hurry;

17. *Annals of the Congress of the United States*, 6th Cong., 2d sess., 1800, col. 613.

but when you come before a committee, sir, to give information as to a very important matter that the public is entitled to know about, unless it goes to the question of endangering the public welfare, it seems to me that you waive the right you claim now, as the President—

GENERAL BRADLEY. Senator, it seems to me that in my position as an adviser, one of the military advisers to the President, and to anybody else in a position of responsibility who wants it, that if I have to publicize my recommendations and my discussions, that my value as an adviser is ruined.

I may be wrong in this. I will abide by whatever the committee says, but it seems to me that when any of us have to tell everything that we say in our position as an adviser, that we might just as well quit.

SENATOR WILEY. I am not going to ask you to do that.

There is one issue before the bar of public opinion, and only one in this matter, as I see it, others disagree with me, and that is—whether or not this action, taken in the manner it was taken, can be justified by the facts, before the bar of public opinion.

Now, the President exercised the authority he had, constitutionally, but he, sir, agreed to present you before this committee. He had a right to say "NO" to it, you need not come. It seems to me that he has opened up the whole case, and that evidence ought to be given to the people, as to just how it happened that this very unusual and cruel action was taken by the associates of General MacArthur, and by the President of the United States. . . .

GENERAL BRADLEY. May I correct my statement a little bit? I am not too sure that I would have the right to say that I would be guided by this committee.

Maybe I should take this to the President and get his permission to do it because I was acting as his adviser at the time, and I am not sure but what I should get his permission to tell you rather than to take it on myself to say I would do it under any other circumstances. . . .

Ruling of the Chair on Confidential Relationships

CHAIRMAN RUSSELL. . . . I know that in my opinion any conversation with respect to any of my actions that I might

> have, any conference I might have with my administrative assistant in my office I think should be protected, and it is my own view, and I so rule, that any matter that transpired in the private conversation between the President and the Chief of Staff as to detail can be protected by the witness if he so desires, and if General Bradley relies upon that relationship, so far as the Chair is concerned, though I regret very much that the issue was raised and I am compelled to pass on it, I would rule that he be protected.[18]

The vote was eighteen to eight sustaining the ruling of the chair. During this stage of the inquiry, Senator Fulbright indicated that the confidentiality of conversations with a president was defensible under the doctrine of the separation of powers, but he voted not to support Bradley's position.[19] The General did not maintain this grant of immunity. Subsequently he outlined the advice given the president why General MacArthur should have been relieved of his command.[20]

President John F. Kennedy expressed concern about the need for a confidential relationship with his subordinates in 1962 when he directed the secretaries of defense and state not to disclose to a congressional committee the names of "any individual with respect to any particular speech reviewed by him." The inquiry involved military cold war education and speech review policies and, according to then Assistant Attorney General Rehnquist, the president said: "It would not be possible for you to maintain an orderly Department and receive the candid advice and loyal respect of your subordinates if they, instead of you and your senior associates, are to be individually answerable to the Congress, as well as to you, for their internal

18. U.S. Congress, Senate, *Hearings before the Committee on Armed Forces and the Committee on Foreign Relations*, pt. 2, 1st sess., 1951, pp. 762 ff.
19. Ibid., pp. 860, 871.
20. Senate, *Hearings,* 1951, p. 878.

acts and advice."[21] A similar view was expressed by President Nixon in his 1973 statement on the executive privilege. The emphasis by Kennedy and Nixon was on the protection of *advice* given a president by his subordinates.

Extending the executive privilege to advice and its private nature was illustrated earlier in 1948 during the investigation by a special subcommittee of the Committee on Education and Labor of the House of Representatives. The investigation centered upon the Government Services, Inc., strike and sought to determine on what authority and for what reason workers in cafeterias in two government buildings were denied the opportunity to work by having the buildings closed. The inquiry also was concerned with questions of loyalty and failure of union members to file required non-Communist affidavits.[22]

On March 6, 1948, the subcommittee issued a subpoena calling for the appearance of John R. Steelman, then a presidential adviser. Steelman did not appear at the time requested. The chairman of the subcommittee, Representative Claire E. Hoffman of Michigan, then inquired:

> . . . Is he a member of the Cabinet?
>
> MR. REIMAN. He is a Presidential adviser.
>
> MR. HOFFMAN. Find out whether the statute applies to a Presidential adviser, or whether they are exempt from the statutes requiring the average ordinary citizen to appear.
>
> So, ladies and gentlemen, that is all we have tonight. Later you will know whether the Government can command the attendance of individuals who happen to be advisers to the President.[23]

Reviewing this incident in his 1971 testimony, Secretary

21. Rehnquist quoted from an undisclosed letter during testimony in 1971. See Senate, *Hearing*, 1971, p. 433.

22. U.S. Congress, House of Representatives, Committee *Hearings*, 80th Cong., 2d sess., 1948, pp. 347–50.

23. The inquiry was directed to F. Albert Reiman, staff member of the committee.

of State Rogers said that Steelman "in both instances . . . returned the subpena with a letter stating that 'in each instance the President directed me, in view of my duties as his assistant, not to appear before your subcommittee.' "[24]

The advice privilege is fundamental to executive privacy and presidents insist that discussions with advisers must be fully protected. As Hamilton put it, "it is one thing to be subordinate to the laws, and another to be dependent on the legislative body. The first comports with, the last violates, the fundamental principles of good government."[25]

Throughout the history of the presidency, those holding that office have endeavored to follow the recent advice given by Chief Justice Berger and Justice Stewart that there is a constitutional power and duty for a president to protect confidentiality. But they have not always been as successful as they might have desired. Violations of privacy have come from the very subordinates where confidence was to be fully respected.[26]

Not all subordinates have followed the example, cited earlier, of J. Edgar Hoover, who refused even to release a directive from the president respecting the scope of testimony he was not to give a House committee. And no one can reverse a disclosure of confidentiality once made. If the domination of a subordinate is not complete or the loyalty characterized by Chief Justice Taft is not observed, there are remedial measures if only to attempt to prevent future violations.

24. Senate, *Hearing*, 1971, p. 474.

25. *Federalist* no. 71.

26. In *Boske* v. *Comingore*, 177 U.S. 459, 470 (1900), the court said in construing a statute empowering the secretary of the treasury to make regulations involving tax records and their disclosure that "great confusion might arise in the business of the Department if the Secretary allowed the use of records and papers in the custody of collectors to depend upon the discretion or judgment of subordinates."

One of the most celebrated recent instances of alleged violation of executive confidentiality involved the actions of Otto F. Otepka, who, in 1962, in his capacity as the chief of the Evaluation Division of the Department of State Office of Security, testified before the Internal Security Subcommittee in apparent violation of a presidential directive. His testimony involved charges that the security measures in the department were relaxed and not effective. The department's position was that the president's directive "removes from the purview of the individual employee's judgment the many questions that may arise" in any disclosure of information. Otepka reportedly favored stricter and more detailed procedures in granting security clearances and gave out documents to the subcommittee's chief counsel.

The result was that Otepka was given a dismissal order on November 5, 1963, not only for his testimony and the giving out of documents, but also because he allegedly had declassified some documents and mutilated a confidential document from the department to the president's special assistant on national security affairs. It was also charged that he prepared questions which the subcommittee's chief counsel could use to ask of department witnesses in a case the subcommittee had under inquiry. Otepka claimed that according to law no civil servant could be punished because he furnished information to a committee of the Congress.[27]

Although the executive privilege was in near disuse during the tenure of President Lyndon B. Johnson, it was invoked as a means of preventing an inroad into executive privacy in 1968. During the course of the testimony on

27. *Congressional Quarterly Almanac* (Washington, D.C.: Congressional Quarterly, 1963), p. 1117, and ibid., 1966, p. 1383. On March 19, 1969, President Nixon appointed Otepka to the Subversive Activities Control Board shortly after Secretary Rogers refused to reinstate him to his former position.

the proposed appointment of Justice Abe Fortas to be chief justice of the United States, the Senate Committee on the Judiciary invited Joseph W. Barr, undersecretary of the treasury, and W. De Vier Pierson, associate special counsel to the president, to appear before the committee. Barr replied:

> Dear Mr. Chairman: I have your invitation to appear before the Committee on the Judiciary to testify in the hearings on the nomination of Mr. Justice Fortas to be Chief Justice.
>
> My understanding is that the Committee wishes my testimony concerning the development of legislation authorizing Secret Service protection to Presidential candidates, which was enacted on June 6, 1968 on an urgent basis following the assassination of Senator Robert F. Kennedy. The legislation had been in preparation for some time as a cooperative effort of the Appropriations Committee and the Executive branch.
>
> In the development of this legislation, I participated in meetings with representatives of the White House and discussed the matter directly with the President.
>
> Based on long-standing precedent, it would be improper for me under these circumstances to give testimony before a Congressional committee concerning such meetings and discussions. Therefore, I must, with great respect, decline your invitation to appear and testify.[28]

Pierson refused on the grounds that he was a member of the president's immediate staff, replying in part:

> . . . It has been firmly established as a matter of principle and precedents, that members of the President's immediate staff shall not appear before a Congressional committee to testify with respect to the performance of their duties on behalf of the President. This limitation, which has been recognized by the Congress as well as the Executive, is fundamental to our system of government. I must, therefore,

28. Quoted in House, *Hearings . . . on Government Operations*, 1972, pt. 8, *Problems of Congress in Obtaining Information from the Executive Branch*, p. 1347.

respectfully decline the invitation to testify in these hearings.[29]

One of the first conflicts over executive privacy in the first Nixon term stemmed from a request from the Senate Committee on Foreign Relations for a copy of a report on Vietnam prepared for the president's use.[30] The report had been prepared by Sir Robert Thompson. The committee received this reply from the assistant secretary for congressional relations: "I regret it is not possible to comply with your request. Sir Roberts' most recent report, as was the case with the earlier one, was prepared for the President personally. Thus, in line with the Administration's policy, in such instances and our reply to your request of last December the report is not being made available to the Congress nor to the public."

This refusal prompted the committee chairman to observe that Thompson "is not a citizen of this country nor is he on the staff nor could he be considered a Presidential advisor in the same terms that Mr. House was or Mr. Hopkins."

In his memorandum to Secretary of Defense Laird of August 31, 1971, President Nixon said that to provide information which was requested about military assistance planning would "not be in the public interest" and to give it would "impair the orderly function of the executive branch." He also stated that unless the "privacy of preliminary exchange of views between personnel of the executive branch can be maintained, the full, frank and healthy expression of opinion which is essential for the successful administration of government would be muted."[31]

29. Ibid., p. 1348.

30. Senate, *Hearing*, 1971, p. 477.

31. In his March 12, 1973 statement on the executive privilege, the president said that his "staff members must not be inhibited by the possibility that their advice and assistance will ever become a matter of public debate, either during their tenure in Government or at a later date." Sixteen days later, however, a former presidential aide presented

These expressions in the support of executive privacy were endorsed some years earlier during the Senate debate over the Freedom of Information Act when Senator Hubert H. Humphrey of Minnesota said of employees of the executive branch that "the knowledge that their views might be made public information would interfere with the freedom of judgment of agency employees and color their views accordingly. Memorandums summarizing facts used as a basis for recommendations would likewise appear to be excluded."[32] And the Senate committee report on the measure included these comments: "It was argued, and with merit, that efficiency of Government would be greatly hampered if, with respect to legal and policy matters, all Government agencies were prematurely forced to 'operate in a fishbowl.'"[33]

A House committee report on the act also supported the need for privacy in the executive branch.

> If agency decisions by superiors are to be made with the benefit of full, frank, and open discussion, and recommendations by and between subordinates, these comments and recommendations must have the protection of privileged information. Otherwise, every memorandum would be carefully written with a view toward its possible impact on the public. . . . The difficulty of writing a memorandum of law or policy without including factual matters would have the effect of either denying the privilege to many memorandums that should be protected or prompting artificial memorandums splitting, with factual memoran-

memoranda in a civil service hearing which dealt with White House discussions about the dismissal of A. Ernest Fitzgerald from his position in the Department of the Air Force. The president was quoted as saying that he was "totally aware" of the possible dismissal. (*New York Times*, March 29, 1973).

32. *Congressional Record*, 88th Cong., 2d sess., p. 17667.

33. Quoted in the solicitor general's brief in *Environomental Protection Agency* v. *Mink*, op. cit., p. 36.

dums cross-referenced to policy or legal memorandums on the same subject.[34]

During the 1971 inquiry about the executive privilege one witness spoke of the deliberative processes and their private nature.

> . . . finally, a word concerning the most difficult and perhaps most deceptive grounds asserted for the privilege: the protection of the internal deliberative processes of the executive branch. In theory it can be readily defended. It is not difficult to perceive that the power of Congress to scrutinize the opinions, the recommendations, the thinking processes, of the executive could inhibit the giving of candid and unpopular advice and the exercise of independent judgment, and in so doing render the Executive wholly subservient to Congress. . . . Yet, this is potentially a most mischievious privilege. Virtually every scrap of paper written in the executive branch can, if desired, be labeled an internal working paper. . . . Rarely are matters neatly labeled "facts," "opinions" "advice." It can be used as readily to shield opinion corrupted by graft and disloyalty as to protect candor and honest judgment.[35]

During the initial phases of the Senate inquiry into alleged election irregularities in the 1972 presidential campaign it was claimed by critics that executive privilege, if extended to White House staff members, was designed to "shield opinion corrupted by graft."

Although President Lyndon B. Johnson invoked executive privilege sparingly, one of his aides testified about it during the 1971 inquiry. George Reedy, one-time press secretary to Johnson, gave this view about executive deliberations:

> When I look at this question of executive privilege, I, myself, cannot see any real objection to assuming that a President is a person who cannot be touched, cannot be sum-

34. Ibid., p. 37. It could be construed that papers have greater protection from disclosure than would testimony.

35. Senate, *Hearing*, 1971, p. 249.

> moned, . . . as a practical matter, there is nothing that can be done about it anyway. He is the head of an equal and coordinate branch of the Government and if a President wants to be stiff-necked about it, if he himself really wishes to withhold information, I think Congress can make his life uncomfortable, but I do not think that Congress has the ultimate power to compel him to act; whether for good reasons, for bad reasons, arbitrarily, capriciously, or wisely, or any other way.
>
> . . . I doubt very much whether any legislation can be devised that will compel the disclosure of all information within the executive branch. . . . I have heard some arguments that to give the President this sort of task is also conceding to him the doctrine of executive privilege. I do not mind it too much, simply because I do not think there is anything that can be done about it. I think he can exercise it merely by the fact of his position.[36]

But Reedy made one reservation which, if followed, would restrict the exercise of executive privilege to the president himself. It should not be claimed by subordinates. The president, according to his analysis, can protect the privacy of his deliberations since "there will always be some things about which Presidents will not speak."

Raoul Berger, on the other hand, insisting that a president does not have any self-determined right to maintain the privacy of deliberations, nonetheless doubted that congressional action could be successful in imposing restraints on the exercise of executive privilege. "I trust you can come to grips with the problem; that you want a solution, that you want to get a chance to decide whether the President does indeed have uncontrolled discretion to withhold information and so bring an intolerably prolonged controversy to an end. And I submit to you, gentlemen, that the only way you can do that is via the courts."[37]

Recourse to a judicial determination was suggested by

36. Ibid., pp. 456, 460.
37. Ibid., p. 286.

President Nixon in March, 1973, following adverse reaction to his statement on the executive privilege which would deny appearances of presidential aides in the course of congressional inquiries. Nixon said, "We think that the Supreme Court will uphold, as it always usually has, the great constitutional principle of separation of powers rather than to uphold the Senate."[38]

As a means of preventing or more effectively controlling disclosures of confidentiality in the executive branch, the Department of State in 1971 warned overseas staffs that "reports of dissent by younger officers must not be allowed to leak to Congress or to the press." The warning reportedly was sent under a restricted distribution, but that report itself was disclosed and confirmed by an unidentified Foreign Service officer. The warning was intended to prevent having "dissenting views leak all over town. If Foreign Service officers disagree they should do so inside the shop—and not go running to the press or to Congress so that these dissents can be picked up and used by the President's political opponents."[39]

Some months later, an assistant attorney general told a House armed forces subcommittee that "administrative and criminal sanctions may attach to the unauthorized release of secret national security documents." The type of sanctions was not indicated, but this episode is evidence of the problem the executive branch faced and the methods suggested to try to prevent unauthorized release of information. It is doubtful that violations of confidences in documents and papers would bring criminal sanctions unless they had a security classification. Other sanctions

38. The statement was made at the time of the Senate Special Committee to Investigate the Watergate affair involving the break-in and other illegal acts at Democratic National Headquarters in 1972. The committee, in its 1973 investigation, was seeking testimony from White House counsel John W. Dean III.

39. *New York Times*, November 21, 1971.

could include reprimand, demotion, transfer, or even dismissal. These are often effective deterrents.[40]

In the Congress, on the other hand, strong efforts were undertaken early in 1973 to force the immediate subordinates of the president to testify before congressional committees when requested to do so. The Senate Democratic caucus resolved to force "Cabinet officers and other officials" to testify when called or face possible contempt charges. The action was designed to limit the exercise of executive privilege and arose because of a belief that the Congress, for some time, had been told too little of what was being done in the executive branch. Senator Ervin said that the privilege was being abused to the point that "almost a file clerk could invoke the privilege."[41]

The caucus resolution would recognize the privilege only if the president "expressly pleads in writing" that he wishes to invoke it. Not only would the resolution attempt to force the personal and direct intervention by the president, it would leave to the discretion of the committee involved whether the president's position was proper. If not, then a report would be made to the full Senate, where disposition would be made and a determination whether to proceed with a contempt citation.

Although President Nixon stated that he had invoked the executive privilege only three times during his first term in office, the equivalent has been extended or has produced the same result. Whether at the formal direction of the president or not, some invitations to testify were ignored or only restricted testimony given by Secretary Rogers, Secretary John Volpe, and Secretary George Romney. The president's adviser for national security affairs, Dr. Kissinger, refused to honor invitations to testify, but reportedly met many times with members of the Senate Committee on Foreign Relations on an informal basis.

40. Subject to statutory provisions and appropriate regulations.

41. *New York Times*, January 19, 1973.

These arrangements are selective, however, and do not answer the demand that the Congress should be permitted to share in the formation of secrets.[42]

At the beginning of the second Nixon term in 1973, the president announced a number of changes in executive positions. In doing so, he made some dual assignments for some members of the cabinet. In addition to a cabinet post, a companion assignment on the White House staff was given to Secretary of Agriculture Earl L. Butz as counselor for natural resources. Secretary of Health, Education, and Welfare Caspar Weinberger was made counselor for human resources, and Secretary of Housing and Urban Development James T. Lynn was appointed as counselor for community development. In the cabinet position each was required to have Senate consent, but as White House counselors no Senate approval is required.[43]

This arrangement immediately raised the question in the Congress whether mixed assignments could be used to restrict testimony if those cabinet members were called. Were the two assignments so intertwined that the shield of the executive privilege would be unduly extended?

In considering the nomination of Secretary Elliott L. Richardson to the Department of Defense, the Senate committee asked him for his views on the 1972 bombing of North Vietnam, but he refused to reveal them. He did not claim any separate status or privilege, but the tenor of the inquiry indicated the conflict which may arise when a secretary is engaged in confidential discourse with the president.

42. *National Observer*, January 27, 1973.

43. The organizational arrangement directed by the president was intended to accomplish the reorganization plan which was submitted in 1971 but not enacted. The dual role as counselors was short-lived. It was abandoned in May, 1973, at least temporarily, pending congressional consideration of a 1973 reorganizational plan. The abandonment, however, was likely prompted by a desire to improve scarred presidential relations with the Congress.

Similarly, Claude S. Brinegar, chosen to be secretary of transportation, would not commit himself on whether he believed that urban highway funds should be used to build mass transit systems. He indicated that he expected to be the president's chief adviser on transportation matters even though that was a responsibility for the department.[44]

An encounter in the dual role came on February 1, 1973, when Secretary Butz refused to testify before a Senate panel on the president's impounding of appropriated funds. Presumably, the refusal was based on grounds that any discussion about the reasons for the impounding was done in his role as counselor and was therefore private.[45]

These encounters with cabinet officers prompted the preparation and release of the president's statement on the executive privilege on March 12, 1973. As indicated above, the statement specified the dual roles assigned to some officers and restricted their testimony in their White House roles.

Critics of the doctrine of executive privilege and the need for executive privacy often assert that any present or former practice of the craft is self-serving. True or not, the testimony in 1971 by former secretary of state Dean Rusk gives some further insight into the need for privacy.

> You know, when your President tells you that he is very reluctant to invoke executive privilege you try to avoid the situation as much as you can. For example, in public session I would sometimes say that involves a matter of such sensitivity that we ought to discuss that in a closed session. And there were times in closed sessions when some Member of Congress would ask me about a private talk that I might have had with the President. And I would say, well, now I wonder if on reflection in our system that conversations

44. *New York Times*, January 10, 1973.

45. Some accommodation was reached after Senator Ervin threatened to subpoena the secretary.

between the President and his Cabinet officers are privileged, and I don't know if you want to go into that.

There are times when you can provide information quietly which you might not feel entitled to provide constitutionally. And I have had the experience of giving information to some Members of Congress who have said to me, gee, I wish you hadn't told me that. . . .

Senator, I might suggest that what are normally called secrets are a very tiny fraction of the public business. And I would hazard the observation that I really don't know of any secrets which have a significant bearing upon the ability of the public to make their judgments about major issues of policy. . . .

Then we have other kinds of information that is not secret in the political sense, but simply involves privacy. I would suppose that a Senator and a Congressman have a right to have a private conversation with the Secretary of State and not have the Secretary of State going around and talking about that either in Congress or anywhere else. . . .

You don't make public your discussions with your colleagues in the corridors and in their offices, you don't make public the communications you have with all your constituents about their views on pending legislation or their needs from the various departments of Government.

So there is a big range of privacy, which is not pejorative, which is not evil or cynical or suspicious, but simply because it is private.[46]

It could be concluded that the president and his chief subordinates have a right of privacy "greater than that of mere citizens," but under what conditions and to what extent this privacy will be generally recognized and supported remains debatable.[47] To the extent that privacy is honored, there is an unfettered atmosphere for the kind of deliberations a president wishes to maintain. There

46. Senate, *Hearing*, 1971, pp. 346, 347.

47. Senator Ervin said on April 1, 1973, in response to the president's refusal to permit White House counsel Dean to testify that he was not willing to elevate a White House aide above the great masses of the American people.

should be no debate that a president needs access to all available choices. These may include suggestions which might be wholly intolerable and unacceptable, and if so, that further strengthens the need that deliberations be done in confidence.

A president is a *political* executive and avoiding *political* antagonisms is one of his prerogatives. If privacy in deliberations, including interagency advice, cannot be maintained, there could be the tendency, frequently expressed, that subordinates would restrict substantially the alternatives they may cause to be brought to the president's attention or would be restrained from presenting views in the selection of choices which might later be the object of legislative inquiry.

In *Soucie* v. *David*, the circuit court of appeals for the District of Columbia in a concurring opinion by Judge Wilkey gave this advice:

> Conceiveably on remand the trial court may also reach a question of constitutional privilege. To put this question in perspective, it must be understood that the privilege against disclosure of the decision-making process is a tripartite privilege, because precisely the same privilege in conducting certain aspects of public business exists for the legislative and judicial branches as well as for the executive. It arises from two sources, one common law and the other constitutional.
>
> Historically, and apart from the Constitution, the privilege against public disclosure to other coequal branches of the Government arises from the common sense–common law principle that not all public business can be transacted completely in the open, that public officials are entitled to the private advice of their subordinates and to confer among themselves freely and frankly, without fear of disclosure. Otherwise the advice received and the exchange of views may not be as frank and honest as the public good requires.
>
> . . . The constitutional part of the privilege arises from the principle of the separation of powers among the legisla-

tive, executive and judicial branches of our Government.[48]

Presidents will seek to maintain privacy and endeavor to secure it by whatever means they possess. Efforts both inside and outside the government to breach that privacy likely will correspondingly mount as the executive presses to prevent invasions into its deliberations. Professor Alexander N. Bickel has said that the contest is a "game" and one which may result in unruly accommodation.[49] Whether unruly or not and whether or not it is played within some recognized rules, a president knows that as means are devised to prevent disclosures about deliberations and discussions it will not result in closing the prospects of disclosures even by stealth and theft.

48. Op. cit., 1080, 1081. The action was dismissed, however, by the district court on August 30, 1971.

49. *New York Times*, February 27, 1973.

VI

Policing the Privilege

The executive privilege was invoked infrequently between World Wars I and II. It was extended to the London Treaty by President Hoover in 1930. Franklin D. Roosevelt's terms show several claims of privilege but few which appear to have been directed by the president himself. As has been shown, the privilege was invoked by Presidents Truman, Eisenhower, and Kennedy, but fell into near disuse under Johnson.[1] At the close of the first Nixon term, executive privilege had been formally invoked by the president three times, but at the beginning of the second term it had become an issue of major proportions between the president and the Congress.

As executive privilege has been extended by presidents to include a variety of situations, efforts have been made in the Congress to constrict it. Some of these efforts have taken legislative form, but few have been successfully concluded. But all of them demonstrate that there are deep

1. A listing is in the *Congressional Record*, 86th Cong., 1st sess., p. 19286, for the period through 1947. The Rogers *Memorandums*, 1958, include the period from 1948 to April 3, 1952. The Eisenhower terms are considered in Kramer and Marcuse, "Executive Privilege." The Kennedy, Johnson, and first Nixon terms are recorded in the *Congressional Record* for March 28, 1973, 93d Cong., 1st sess., pp. H2242–46. The variations in the uses of the executive privilege may be explained partially by the kinds of relationships each president had with the Congress and the nature of the issues.

concerns in the Congress that the president goes too far in the uses of the privilege. Only a minority denies some propriety for the privilege. The results are that as each case has arisen some understandings have been reached so that information requested is given in whole or in part or in some manner, or testimony is given with or without restrictions. These accommodations do not satisfy either the president or the Congress and legislative proposals appear from time to time intended to police or to brake the privilege.

These conflicts between the executive and legislative branches are not surprising, nor are they of a crisis nature, at least not frequently. The executive wants to pursue his tasks without interruptions or attempted diversions from the Congress. Members of the Congress insist that the legislative function and the obligations the Congress has to the people, including oversight of administration, cannot be properly accomplished if documents and testimony from the executive branch are not forthcoming. But when they are requested and given or requested and denied, it is a matter of judgment whether the requests were proper and needed. Equally it is a matter of judgment whether the denials were proper.

Testimony in 1971 about the executive privilege sheds light on the nature of the conflict.

> The problem of executive privilege arises primarily in those areas in which congressional demands for information clash with the President's responsibility to keep the same information secret. Senator Fulbright suggested in his introductory statement that Congress cannot be expected to "abdicate to 'executive caprice' in determining whether or not the Congress will be permitted to know what it needs to know in order to discharge its constitutional responsibilities." But can the executive conversely be required to abdicate to "congressional caprice" and release to Congress information which in the view of the President should not be made public? This conflict becomes all the more serious

because some members of Congress claim the right to determine not only what information should be made available to Congress, but also whether that information once made available to it should be released to the public.[2]

The controversy involves several fundamental issues. One of these is timing. When is the privilege to be invoked and, often, to whose advantage? What type of information is to be given or withheld and under what conditions? Who in the executive branch may invoke it, or if it is to be invoked only by the president, to whom can he extend it? Further, in what manner is the privilege to be presented or invoked?

When the Senate, in 1930, was not able to obtain memoranda requested associated with the negotiations for the London Treaty, it chose a policing method to ensure, in its opinion, that the provisions of the treaty as presented included all stipulations and agreements and that no secret understandings had been made and not reflected in the language itself. The Senate response was in the form of a reservation to the treaty.

> That in ratifying said treaty the Senate does so with the distinct and explicit understanding that there are no secret files, documents, letters, understandings, or agreements which in any way, directly or indirectly, modify, change, add to, or take away from any of the stipulations, agreements, or statements in said treaty; and that the Senate ratifies said treaty with the distinct and explicit understanding that, excepting the agreement brought about through the exchange of notes between the Governments of the United States, Great Britain, and Japan having reference to Article XIX, there is no agreement, secret or otherwise, expressed or implied, between any of the parties to said treaty as to any construction that shall hereafter be given to any statement or provision contained therein.[3]

The Senate wanted to give public view to the papers and records involved in the negotiation and the president

2. Senate, *Hearing*, 1971, p. 430.

3. *Congressional Record*, 71st Cong., 2d sess., p. 12029. The vote in the Senate was 58–9.

refused because disclosure of their substance would violate the confidence by which they were obtained.[4] There was not a total denial of access, however, since the president authorized individual members of the Senate to read them. Some did, but this did not find agreement for the majority of the members. What was wanted was the reasoning for the stipulations in the treaty and how they were arrived at.

During the early 1970s an exchange occurred about the conduct of foreign relations and centered upon the number of advisers to the president. Senator Fulbright said, "Unlike Colonel House and Harry Hopkins, who had no staffs of their own, and even unlike Mr. Rostow, who at the end of 1968 had a substantial staff of no more than 12 persons, Mr. Kissinger presides over a staff of 54 'substantive officers' and a total staff of 140 employees."[5] Fulbright considered that it was proper and desirable for a president to have confidential, personal advisers, but not in such numbers. The tensions which developed were heightened because of Kissinger's refusal to meet in formal, even if closed, session with the Senate Committee on Foreign Relations.[6] Members of the committee considered this to be a form of executive branch blackout, and especially so since it denied the Senate the exercise of its power to advise the president on foreign affairs. In the exercise of its advice power the committee wanted to inquire into the reasons for some executive actions and in the process would be consulting with the executive in their respective roles.[7]

The role sought, however, was one of adversary with unwilling witnesses and with no judge to deny the propri-

4. *Congressional Record*, Special Session of the Senate, July 1930, p. 378.

5. Senate, *Hearing*, 1971, p. 21.

6. Ibid., p. 23.

7. Fulbright also stated that the president was not "at liberty to create—nor is Congress at liberty to accept—a policymaking system which undercuts congressional oversight and the advisory role of the Senate in the making of foreign policy" (ibid., p. 22).

ety of questions. When presidents have authorized restricted testimony from subordinates, it has been the president who assumed the responsibility of judging, albeit in advance, the propriety of questions. As Senator Lloyd M. Bentsen, Jr., of Texas said early in 1973, "We want to understand the rationale and the logic behind decisions."[8]

Publicized commentary to the contrary, the majority of the members of the Congress seem generally satisfied with responses to requests for information from the executive branch. What has not been satisfying, however, is the lapse of time, the seeming endless negotiations to obtain information, and particularly when the information does not involve international affairs or national security.[9] It is reported that departments and agencies comply reluctantly or not at all with congressional requests and without any attempt at promptness. In some instances the information wanted, when received long after the request was made, has been found to be of no great value since the reasons which prompted the request were no longer current.[10]

The obvious dissatisfaction resulting from this conduct has prompted the search for policing methods and regula-

8. *New York Times*, January 18, 1973.

9. In his testimony before the subcommittee of the Committee on Government Operations, House of Representatives, in 1971, one witness said:

> It is no doubt true that the Government must have some secrets. The President must talk to other heads of state in private. He must enjoy confidentiality with his aides and Department heads. The military must keep certain strategic and operational information classified.
>
> But the real need for secrecy on a limited set of facts and plans should not be expanded to suppress vast amounts of information that the people need to know to determine whether they are being governed wisely. [House, *Hearing . . . on Government Operations*, 1972, p. 279.]

10. Senate, *Hearing*, 1971, pp. 479 ff.

tions by the Congress. They are not new, of course, but the objectives are to ensure that if there is not total compliance in honoring requests for documents or testimony, there will be adequate compliance or that noncompliance will be severely restricted.[11]

The policing method in longest use has been that of a simple resolution or a letter of invitation for documents or for appearances. The result has been general compliance. Whether responses during testimony have been satisfying varies, and often testimony is given in whole or in part in closed or executive sessions of committees. On occasion, agreements are reached as to the questions to be asked, as when a presidential aide has been requested to testify. When presidential aide Peter Flanigan agreed to appear before a Senate committee, it was to answer only certain questions previously presented. This arrangement did not satisfy all members of the committee, but the accommodation made did prevail. The request for his appearance was agreed to in order to prevent a more extensive inquiry which threatened the confirmation of Richard G. Kleindienst as attorney general.[12]

Resolutions are couched in brief but formal language. Letters of invitation take a similar form. But these requests may be accompanied by indications that unless documents are forthcoming or testimony is given, then other actions may result. The "other actions" may take the form of well-publicized denials of the right of the executive branch to refuse, or even that the executive privilege has any basis at all. At the time of the Kleindienst hearings, Senator

11. In his "Memorandum for the Heads of Executive Departments and Agencies" of March 24, 1969, President Nixon said that the policy of "this Administration is to comply to the fullest possible extent with Congressional requests for information." But he also indicated that information would be withheld if its release would be "incompatible with the public interest" (Senate, *Hearing*, 1971, p. 36).

12. The letter denying an appearance from presidential counsel John W. Dean, dated April 10, 1972, is included in the Appendix, sec. VII.

Ervin voiced a position about the privilege which, if observed, would have sharply narrowed its uses in recent decades.

> I also think that any communication between an executive officer and third persons is not protected by the executive privilege. I recognize the validity of executive privilege when it is limited to its proper scope. The executive privilege exists only to protect the secrecy of communications between Presidential aides and the President or communications which are exclusively between the executive officials when they are assisting the President in the performance of their duties involved upon him . . . and I think that the recent claim that has been asserted that executive privilege forbids a Presidential aide, just because he is a Presidential aide, from appearing before a congressional committee finds no warrant in the executive privilege properly interpreted and applied.[13]

Reactions of this kind serve as forceful restraints on the exercise of executive privilege. They invite charges that refusals are made to avoid exposure of wrongdoing or political embarrassment. They lead to nation-wide attention via television, radio, and newspaper reports and commentary. Statements or headlines stating, "Trouble for Nixon over Executive Privilege Use," or "A Dubious Secret," or "Aide Refusing to Talk Should be Arrested," make forceful impressions upon the public at large.[14]

Listener or reader impact may be less significant when refusals are not highlighted, but some adverse reaction results from statements such as that by Senator Clifford

13. It was alleged that a pledge of money for the Republican National Convention, originally scheduled for San Diego in 1972, was one of the factors influencing the department's decision in the settlement with the International Telephone and Telegraph Company. Senator Ervin's comment is found in the Senate, *Hearings*, 1971, p. 1414.

14. Sharply couched exchanges between Senator Ervin and White House press secretary Ronald L. Ziegler were given wide coverage throughout the media on April 2, 1973, over the president's refusal to permit testimony from his aides.

P. Case of New Jersey in 1972 about the U.S. Information Agency and may be an effective brake on refusals to give information. Case said that his committee "could not pass on the agency's budget unless it had access to basic information about the program."[15] Similarly, the public reaction may be adverse to the exercise of privilege after a comment such as that in 1971 by Senator Fulbright that Secretary Rogers had "all too often withheld information" from his Committee on Foreign Relations.[16]

When White House counsel Dean, writing on behalf of the president, refused to permit himself and some White House associates to testify about the destructive occupation of the Bureau of Indian Affairs Building in 1972, one political commentary was that "Dean invoked executive privilege, but his true reasons are steeped in politics. The White House knows it will get a black eye out of the congressional investigation and, therefore, is desperately trying to separate Mr. Nixon from the government's handling of the BIA occupation."[17]

In the nuclear test controversy, news comment put the question as one not "whether the Government need fear 'stories harmful to the national interest,' but whether the national interest can stand much more of this excessive concealment of information."[18]

How effective these reports and commentaries are in limiting the exercise of executive privilege is not easily determined, but they are not without some influence. Presidents know of these reactions and know that they may produce deep distrust of government. They also do not want to have a place in history which would be degrading. Thus, a president will weigh carefully the effects of the use of executive privilege.

Since programs require funding, restricting or refusing

15. *New York Times*, March 21, 1972.

16. Ibid., March 5, 1971.

17. *Lincoln Evening Journal*, November 27, 1972.

18. *New York Times*, September 7, 1971.

appropriations when requested information is not forthcoming is an effective means of policing the privilege. This occurred in 1971, for example, when the Senate Appropriations Committee said it would not provide funding for foreign military assistance unless a projection of needs was given to it. The result was that Secretary Rogers met privately with committee members and gave some wanted information. Senator Gale W. McGee of Wyoming said at the time that unless the material was furnished, "we are not going to have a foreign aid bill because there is not going to be an authorization."[19]

When the 92d Congress adjourned in October, 1972, a bill for foreign aid appropriations died in conference as a result of a difference over Senate-approved amendments requiring Senate approval of executive agreements.[20] The issue was not whether financial support should be extended, although the Senate had defeated a foreign aid bill in the previous year, but rather a provision which would require that an agreement with Portugal for an air base in the Azores Islands be presented to the Senate in the form of a treaty. This was opposed by the president. A companion proposal to cut off funds to support 1971 executive agreements with Portugal and Bahrain died because no final action was taken.[21]

The extensive use of executive agreements instead of treaties since 1930 has heightened a conflict between the president and the Senate, since under the Constitution the Senate gives its "advice and consent" to treaties to make them effective and binding. Executive agreements do not

19. *Lincoln Evening Journal*, September 8, 1971.

20. On February 28, 1973, financing was extended by resolution to June 30, 1973.

21. The text of the Senate measure is included in the Appendix, sec. VIII. Senate conferees offered to drop a provision dealing with the Portuguese agreement and to require approval by simple majorities of both houses instead of the two-thirds majority of the Senate as in the case of treaties, but the Senate would not agree.

require Senate sanction and in practice are not published. A report indicates that as of January, 1969, the United States was a party to 909 treaties and 3,973 executive agreements. In 1968 alone the United States entered into 16 treaties and more than 200 executive agreements.[22]

Objections to the use of executive agreements have been raised frequently that they may contain commitments which could lead to U.S. involvement in international conflicts. In 1950 legislation was approved directing the secretary of state to compile and publish annually the contents of all treaties and executive agreements made during the preceding year, but since many of the agreements were given a classification status, they were not made available even on a confidential basis. The statute provides:

> The Secretary of State shall cause to be compiled, edited, indexed, and published, beginning as of January 1, 1950, a compilation entitled "United States Treaties and Other International Agreements," which shall contain all treaties to which the United States is a party that have been proclaimed during each calendar year, and all international agreements other than treaties to which the United States is a party that have been signed, proclaimed, or with reference to which any other final formality has been executed, during each calendar year. The said United States Treaties and Other International Agreements shall be legal evidence of the treaties, international agreements other than treaties, and proclamations by the President of such treaties and agreements, therein contained, in all the courts of the United States, the several states, and the Territories and insular possessions of the United States.[23]

To overcome the withholding of agreements which were confidential and carried a security classification, the Congress passed legislation which was approved by the president requiring the submission of the texts of agree-

22. *CQ*, 1972, p. 458.
23. *U.S. Code*, Title I, sec. 112a.

ments to the appropriate committees of the House and the Senate.

> The Secretary of State shall transmit to the Congress the text of any international agreement, other than a treaty, to which the United States is a party as soon as practicable after such agreement has entered into force with respect to the United States but in no event later than sixty days thereafter. However, any such agreement the immediate public disclosure of which would, in the opinion of the President, be prejudicial to the national security of the United States shall not be so transmitted to the Congress but shall be transmitted to the Committee on Foreign Relations of the Senate and the Committee on Foreign Affairs of the House of Representatives *under an appropriate injunction of secrecy to be removed only upon due notice from the President.*[24]

This 1972 statute was designed to overcome the lack of compliance by the executive branch with the one enacted in 1950. It is significant also since it extends into the field of international affairs, wherein the executive branch had been the only participant. To make the measure palatable to the president and to recognize the problems of public release which might violate not only the wishes of participating nations, but also the national defense and security of the United States, the president would send the texts not to the Congress, but to the appropriate House and Senate committees "under an appropriate injunction of secrecy."

During the debate over the measure in the House, Representative Clement J. Zablocki of Wisconsin said that "to keep them entirely secret from the Congress is a distortion of our constitutional system. Yet, that is what happened in the past and may well happen in the future" unless the proposal was enacted into law. And as Senator Ervin said at the time, "if the executive branch . . . is entirely free to determine what it will submit to the Senate in this

24. *Public Law 92–403*. Emphasis supplied.

area, then the constitutional provision requiring Senate participation in the treaty-making field is no more than a piece of dead parchment." Senator Bentsen commented that the measure would not weaken the president's powers and that the Congress could not be put in a position of "accepting on blind trust" that a chief executive or his aide, "shielded by executive privilege, is somehow omniscient and omnipotent and always knows best."[25]

Senator Fulbright declared that approval of the measure in no way "gives validity to such agreements, which . . . should be treaties." To him the "Constitution did not anticipate that matters of this importance should be done by executive agreement."[26]

Concern was expressed at the time of Senate approval that the measure would have an adverse impact on executive prerogatives. Senator Roman L. Hruska of Nebraska, ranking minority member of the Senate Committee on the Judiciary, told the Senate that he believed further study was needed on the proposal and "whether there is danger that we could invade the doctrine of the separation of powers which applies to some aspects of the executive department's function." He supported the view that disclosure would end the confidence afforded by the executive privilege and that the provision for congressional consideration of the documents was highly suspect. He declared that

> anyone who has served in the Congress any small number of years—they do not have to be great in number—knows there is very little assurance that secrecy will prevail. In fact, the opposite is true. Here we would be dealing with the number of those serving on the committee in this body and also with the larger number who are in the relevant committee in the other body. There would be no assurance that the secrecy would be inviolably kept, and if it is a particularly

25. *Congressional Record*, 92d Cong., 2d sess., pp. H7578, S1909.
26. Ibid., p. S1909.

> sensitive executive agreement, that might spell trouble for this country.[27]

Nonetheless, the measure became law with the president's approval when he signed it on August 22, 1972.

The hearings in 1971 by the Senate Subcommittee on Separation of Powers of the Committee on the Judiciary were prompted by Senator Fulbright's bill which would require appearances, documents, and testimony from anyone in the executive branch of the government. If anyone who appeared asserted the executive privilege, a statement would have to be signed personally by the president supporting its use. Furthermore, the letter from the president would have to outline his reasons for invoking the privilege with respect to the information requested. If a letter was not forthcoming, the information would have to be given within thirty days after the request was made. If this requirement was not met, then no funds appropriated to the agency or office would be available for obligation or expenditure beginning on the seventieth day following the request.

In his statement to the subcommittee on July 27, 1971, Senator Fulbright gave at least tacit recognition that there was a constitutional basis for the executive privilege. He said that his purpose was "not to eliminate but to restrict the practice of 'executive privilege,' by reducing it to bounds in which it will cease to interfere with the people's right to know and the Congress's duty to investigate and oversee the execution of the laws." Furthermore, he said that his purpose was to "eliminate the unwarranted extension of the claim of privilege from information to persons." The bill, had it been enacted, "would require an official such as the President's assistant on national security affairs to appear before an appropriate congressional committee if only for the purpose of stating, in effect: 'I have been

27. Ibid., p. S1911.

instructed in writing by the President to invoke executive privilege and here is why * * *.' "[28] This requirement for not only an appearance, but also a letter from the president containing his reasons, is indicative of the strong views held by some of the members of the Senate. It is also recognition that if these appearances occurred and the letter invoking privilege were produced, with reasons, it would be a useless and antagonistic gesture. The letter could be sent without the presence of the official in whose behalf it was to be applied, but forcing an appearance presumably was to dramatize the possibility of an impasse between the president and a congressional committee.[29]

Fulbright's proposal was designed also to restrict executive control over information generally. He told his colleagues that

> the principle would be established that information could be withheld from Congress only on the basis of a formal invocation of executive privilege, in effect, eliminating the all-too-common Executive practice of withholding information on vague and insubstantial grounds, such as the contention that a document is purely a "planning" document, or that it would be "inappropriate" or "contrary to the national interest" to disseminate it more widely.[30]

Other provisions would involve a determination by the attorney general of any need to invoke the privilege, a provision recognized by President Nixon in his 1969 directive.

The Fulbright proposal had a dual purpose. One was to strengthen the influence of the Congress over presidential assistants. The other was to try to prevent or limit the claim of executive privilege by "employees" in the various agencies of the executive branch.

28. Senate, *Hearing*, 1971, p. 20.

29. Cf. the appearance of J. Edgar Hoover in 1944 and his refusal to respond even about the contents of his directive.

30. Senate, *Hearing*, 1971, pp. 20, 21.

The scheme would also delineate the nature of information which the Congress could demand. Information in the custody of an agency would have to be given up "so that the Congress may exercise, in an informed manner, the authority conferred upon it by article I of the Constitution to make laws necessary and proper to carry into execution the powers vested in the Congress and all other powers vested in that Government of any department or officer thereof."[31]

The proposal did not assert any new power for the Congress. But it would place all agencies on notice that some past practices of withholding information could undergo significant changes. It would place the use of the executive privilege by subordinates under some jurisdiction of the attorney general, rather than an agency head. The privilege could not be invoked unless the attorney general recommended it to the president and the latter then invoked it.[32]

The Fulbright measure's provision for noncompliance is not unlike other proposals in providing for the stopping of funds. This raises a question whether the Congress can constitutionally stop funds once an appropriation has been authorized and approved for a particular period of time. It could refuse further appropriations, of course, but forcing the direct appearance of an official and directing the personal participation of the president is plainly hostile.

"No one questions the propriety of executive privilege," Fulbright said, "under certain circumstances; what is and must be contested is the contention that the President alone may determine the range of its application and, in so doing, also determine the range of the Congress' power

31. Ibid., p. 10.

32. One of the problems in enforcing a measure of this kind is the identification of documents or information requested by a committee. Some records may be known to a very few individuals or not suspected to exist. This prompts requests for "all records."

to investigate."[33] If this was the true intent, then the measure, had it been enacted, would be congressional recognition that the executive privilege has a constitutional basis and is not a myth, but it also had overtones that the Congress would be raising a question of the extent of its powers to investigate and compel the production of documents and require testimony.

The senator's plan would not satisfy the critics of executive privilege. Representative Moss claimed that the privilege is an "arrogant claim of the President of the United States" and that the Congress should not recognize it at all. Others object to permitting the president discretion, as would have been authorized, to determine when executive privilege should be invoked. This may have influenced the resolution of the Democratic caucus in 1973 to reserve to the appropriate house the determination whether the reasons for the president's claim to privilege were acceptable.[34]

Another policing method suggested in 1972 would have provided for a cutoff of appropriations for the salaries of any government personnel who refused to testify before a congressional committee. It plainly had overtones of a bill of attainder and was challenged on that ground.[35]

During the 1973 investigations into the 1972 illegal activities which involved the Democratic national headquarters, and which were generally known as the Watergate scandal, charges were made that White House aides not only were knowledgeable about the affair, but also actively participated in planning and directing the illegal entry and surveillance.

Faced with a refusal by the president to permit his aides

33. Senate, *Hearing*, 1971, p. 31.

34. This raises the question whether a president should be able to have confidential advisers protected and have the authority to retain the confidence of their advice or discussions, recorded or not.

35. *Congressional Record*, 92d Cong., 2d sess., p. H6006.

to testify, proposals were renewed in the Congress to rigorously control the exercise of executive privilege by statute or to concurrently encourage a court test through the issue of a subpoena on an aide who presumably would refuse to honor it. Both the president and members of the Congress indicated they would welcome a court test on the privilege, including a decision by the U.S. Supreme Court.[36]

The proposals to control executive privilege included one which would limit it to direct, personal, and confidential relationships between the president and his chief advisers and presumably only on matters involving national security or "other public policy" decisions. Another would specify that the privilege could be invoked only through written notice by the president to the Congress. Still another would set forth procedures to permit judicial review of the validity of the circumstances surrounding the uses of the privilege.[37]

These proposals, however, would recognize executive privilege and more particularly the advice privilege. They indicate that not all confidences would be inviolate unless matters under inquiry had directly involved the president personally. Presumably if the information or testimony requested had been developed by or for the president it would not be subject to uncontrolled examination.

Other ways to police the executive privilege need com-

36. It was observed that the Congress had passed legislation in 1928 designed to compel testimony, but it was limited to the Committees on Government Operations of the House and Senate and did not include White House staff among those affected. See *U.S. Code*, Title V, sec. 2954.

37. House Resolution 4938 of February 28, 1973, included in the Appendix, sec. X, would authorize the president to invoke "Executive privilege" only if he determined that disclosure would seriously jeopardize "the national interest or his ability or that of any agency head to obtain forthright advice." The measure would require that "to the extent possible" any factual information "underlying policy recommendations would have to be made available."

ment. Impeachment is a ready method, but unless personal presidential involvement in wrongdoing is apparent, this would appear a remote route. Yet, the mere threat of impeachment would serve as an indication of the more serious nature of any controversy. An amendment to the Constitution designed to control the privilege or deny it seems equally distant from success.

More clandestine methods have prevailed, however, to circumvent the efforts by the executive to prevent disclosure of information. Undoubtedly Otto F. Otepka would not have been as successful in his disclosures had he not had an eager and willing Senate Judiciary Committee and committee staff who encouraged his testimony. The Judith Coplon disclosures indicate another method which overcame executive controls over information.[38]

Disclosures by individuals in public service made contrary to the known rules of the organization which accepted their confidence and made according to their own standards pose a serious challenge to any policing methods. Any punishment for disclosure in contravention to safeguards would be after the event and after any damage might have resulted; reflecting the difficulty in finding ways to observe Justice Stewart's admonition that executive regulations should be instituted to protect confidentiality.[39]

38. Miss Coplon, a Department of Justice employee, "in early February [1949] went to her successor in the security section, asked to see some of the reports that were filed there, and took away some of them" (*U.S.* v. *Coplon*, 185 F 2d 629, 632 [1950]). When apprehended later, she was carrying in her purse abstracts she had made which were referred to as "data slips." Secretary Rogers reported in his *Memorandums*, 1958, p. 122, that the Department of Justice "took every possible step to prevent disclosure of the information during the trial," but failed. In the "Pentagon Papers" trial in 1972–73, the government claimed that the major issue was a simple case of theft. The case was dismissed on May 11, 1973, leaving the issue unresolved.

39. In 1971 an investigating team known as "the plumbers" attempted to "plug leaks" to the news media by individuals in the executive branch following the publication of the "Pentagon Papers."

Policing methods for the exercise of executive privilege of whatever variety have rarely met with the full satisfaction of the parties involved and are evidence of the issues over the uses of power and the continuing efforts of each of the three branches to settle the boundaries of their respective powers even through occasional confrontation.[40] The author of *Federalist* no. 49 advised, but without specifying a method, that prevention of encroachments of one upon another must come from "an appeal to the people themselves, who, as the grantors of the commission, can alone declare its true meaning, and enforce its observance."

40. When the Congress presented President Nixon on October 10, 1973, with an appropriation measure to support the U.S. Information Agency for fiscal year 1974, it included a provision that if the agency refused to provide *any* information or documents requested by either the Committee on Foreign Relations of the Senate or the Committee on Foreign Affairs of the House, then funds would be cut off after a lapse of thirty-five days. The president vetoed the measure on the ground that it was an unconstitutional attempt on the part of the Congress to undermine the president's constitutional responsibility to withhold information when the disclosure would be contrary to the public interest. The Senate failed in an attempt to override the veto.

VII

Watergate

Issues involving the executive privilege and the separation of powers were intensified when Alexander P. Butterfield, former deputy assistant to President Nixon, disclosed on July 16, 1973, that the president in 1971 had installed various devices in the White House to record conversations.[1] Taped records allegedly included conversations with the president and several of his assistants about the break-in of the Democratic National Headquarters in the Watergate Building in Washington, D.C., and other related events. Because of conflicting testimony given earlier in 1973 before the Senate Select Committee, or Watergate Committee, by John D. Ehrlichman, John W. Dean III, and John N. Mitchell, the committee authorized that subpoenas be issued to obtain the presidential tapes and related records.[2] If the tapes included the alleged conversations, then conflict in testimony about knowledge of the break-in and other illegal acts could be assessed and also, and more importantly, whether the president himself had knowledge of these activities. Since there were claims that the president not only had that knowledge but had known of attempts to prevent disclosure of them, the validity of the assertions could be finally determined.

Thus, this call from the Watergate Committee brought

1. *CQ*, 1973, pp. 1931–34.
2. Ibid., p. 2032.

a new dimension to presidential control over information.[3] As noted above, President Nixon had modified his position on information control by releasing his former assistants from the protection of executive privilege and they had testified. The action to obtain recorded conversations, however, was little short of seeking the direct testimony of the president himself.

Nixon rejected compliance with the request in a letter to Senator Ervin, the committee chairman:

> Dear Mr. Chairman:
>
> White House counsel have received on my behalf the two subpoenas issued by you, on behalf of the Select Committee, on July 23rd.
>
> One of these calls on me to furnish to the Select Committee recordings of five meetings between Mr. John Dean and myself. For the reasons stated to you in my letters of July 6th and July 23rd, I must respectfully refuse to produce those recordings.
>
> The other subpoena calls on me to furnish all records of any kind relating directly or indirectly to the "activities, participation, responsibilities or involvement" of 25 named individuals "in any alleged criminal acts relating to the Presidential election of 1972." Some of the records that might arguably fit within that subpoena are Presidential papers that must be kept confidential for reasons stated in my letter of July 6th. It is quite possible that there are other records in my custody that would be within the ambit of that subpoena and that I could, consistent with the public interest and my Constitutional responsibilities, provide to the Select Committee. All specific requests from the Select Committee will be carefully considered and my staff and I, as we have done in the past, will cooperate with the Select Committee by making available any information and documents that

3. Thomas Jefferson had been served with a subpoena to appear before Chief Justice John Marshall in the Richmond, Virginia, trial of Aaron Burr. Jefferson refused to appear and his action was never challenged. Later he provided some requested information. (*U.S.* v. *Burr*, *op. cit.*, n. 7, p. 4, *supra*.)

can appropriately be produced. You will understand, however, I am sure, that it would simply not be feasible for my staff and me to review thousands of documents to decide which do and which do not fit within the sweeping but vague terms of the subpoena.

It continues to be true, as it was when I wrote you on July 6th, that my staff is under instructions to cooperate fully with yours in furnishing information pertinent to your inquiry. I have directed that executive privilege not be invoked with regard to testimony by present and former members of my staff concerning possible criminal conduct or discussions of possible criminal conduct. I have waived the attorney-client privilege with regard to my former Counsel. In my July 6th letter I described these acts of cooperation with the Select Committee as "genuine, extensive and, in the history of such matters, extraordinary." That cooperation has continued and it will continue. Executive privilege is being invoked only with regard to documents and recordings that cannot be made public consistent with the confidentiality essential to the functioning of the Office of the President.

I cannot and will not consent to giving any investigatory body private Presidential papers. To the extent that I have custody of other documents or information relevant to the work of the Select Committee and that can properly be made public, I will be glad to make these available in response to specific requests.[4]

Subsequently, Judge John J. Sirica of the U.S. District Court for the District of Columbia ruled on October 17,

4. On July 27, 1973, Judge William B. Jones of the U.S. District Court for the District of Columbia directed that memoranda and other documents held by the White House relating to the milk price adjustment of 1971 be provided to him for *in camera* inspection. This was directed over the strong objection of the Department of Justice, which argued that the privacy of the White House's internal communications was essential and protected by executive privilege. The issue arose over allegations that the upward milk price adjustment was in return for milk industry pledges of financial contributions for Nixon's 1972 presidential campaign. See *New York Times*, July 28, 1973.

1973, that the court did not have jurisdiction to entertain a congressional suit against the president and expressed doubt that the constitution makes it an official duty of presidents to comply with congressional subpoenas.

Earlier, on May 18, 1973, arrangements were made in the Department of Justice for a special prosecutor to handle the investigations involving the Watergate allegations and related activities and became a condition for the confirmation of the president's appointment of Elliot L. Richardson, then the Secretary of Defense, to be Attorney General following the resignation of Richard G. Kleindienst.[5] Former Solicitor General Archibald Cox was appointed as special prosecutor with a presumed understanding that he would have independence from executive-branch controls over his endeavors.[6]

Two months after this arrangement was announced, Cox sought access to the presidential tapes. The president refused to release them and Cox issued a subpoena to obtain them. Suit was then entered in the U.S. District Court to seek presidential compliance.

The central issues were whether the president had absolute authority to withhold evidence wanted by a grand jury by a presidential assertion that it was not in the public interest to release it; whether a claim of executive privilege could be invoked to prevent disclosure of possible evidence relating to criminal conduct by government officials and political party leaders; and whether the president had waived executive privilege by previously approved disclosures from the records demanded.[7] Cox argued that the president had an enforceable legal duty to comply and under no circumstances could executive privilege be invoked on either the alleged illegal activities or those relating to the political campaign. Campaign activities, he

5. *CQ*, 1973, p. 1057.

6. Ibid., pp. 1313–15.

7. In its opinion about the disputed tapes, the Court of Appeals said that "the simple fact is that the conversations are no longer confidential."

insisted, were not a constitutional duty and thus not protected.

The president's position was that under the doctrine of the separation of powers the judicial branch did not have authority to direct compliance if he determined that other governmental interests dictated to the contrary. He argued also that the president was not above the law but that he had unique responsibilities and one of these, which was supreme, was presidential privacy. Were the court's decision to be contrary to this position, then courts would compel disclosures at random.

The decision by Judge Sirica on August 29, 1973, disagreed with the president's claim and stated that the judiciary, not the executive, had final authority to determine whether the executive privilege is properly invoked. "The availability of evidence," he said, "including the validity and scope of privileges, is a judicial function." Furthermore, it "is emphatically the province and duty of the judicial department to say what the law is." Sirica disavowed the president's claim of presidential privacy as "not persuasive." The tapes sought by Cox were to be delivered to Sirica for *in camera* inspection because "the court is simply unable to decide the question of privilege without inspecting the tapes." This arrangement, he said, was an "attempt to walk the middle ground between a formula to decide the question of privilege at one extreme, and a wholesale delivery of tapes to the grand jury at the other. The one would be a breach of duty, the other an inexcusable course of conduct."

The middle-ground approach emphasized, however, that separability of privileged information and unprivileged might be impossible, and if material produced is properly the subject of privilege, then even an inspection *in camera* could compromise the privilege. Nevertheless, Sirica said, "it would be an extremely limited infraction and in this case an unavoidable one."

The president appealed this decision, and on September 13, 1973, the U.S. Court of Appeals for the District of Columbia issued a memorandum designed to prevent a constitutional confrontation through some compromise solution between the president and Cox. It was an indication that some accommodation might be reached whereby the president could extricate the privileged and surrender the unprivileged and make the latter available to the grand jury and Cox. An accommodation was not reached, however, and the court ruled on October 12, 1973, that the president should comply with the earlier order of the District Court, but with some modifications to that order.[8] The opinion stated that "to leave the proper scope and application of executive privilege to the President's sole discretion would represent a mixing, rather than a separation, of executive and judicial functions." Seeking to avoid a constitutional crisis, the opinion noted support for confidentiality by the executive.

> We acknowledge that wholesale public access to executive deliberations and documents would cripple the executive as a co-equal branch, but this is an argument for recognizing executive privilege and for according it great weight, not for making the executive the judge of its own privilege. The President's privilege cannot, therefore, be deemed absolute [and] executive privilege depends on a weighing of the public interests that would be served by disclosure in a particular case.

In an apparent effort to support claims for executive privilege in some areas, the opinion contained these words:

> With the possible exception of material on one tape, the

8. There were two dissents in the case. Judge George E. MacKinnon wrote that "the preservation of the confidentiality of the presidential decision-making process is of overwhelming importance to the effective functioning of our three branches of government. Therefore, I would recognize an absolute privilege of confidential presidential communications." Judge Malcolm R. Wilkey said that "if the constitutional privilege has been asserted, then no court has the right to determine what the President will or will not produce."

> President does not assert that the subpoenaed items involve military or state secrets; nor is the asserted privilege directed to the particular kinds of information that the tapes contain. Instead, the President asserts that the tapes should be deemed privileged because of the great public interest in maintaining the confidentiality of conversations that take place in the President's performance of his duties.

The decision of the court was not a blanket directive to produce all information requested. The president was authorized to separate topics and information, retaining some and releasing some. The opinion stated:

> In so far as the President makes a claim that certain material may not be disclosed because the subject matter relates to national defense or foreign relations, he may decline to transmit that portion of the material and ask the district court to reconsider whether in camera inspection of the material is necessary. The special prosecutor is entitled to inspect the claim and showing and may be heard thereon, in chambers. If the judge sustains the privilege, the text of the Government's statement will be preserved in the court's record under seal.
>
> The President will present to the district court all other items covered by the order, with specification of which segments he believes may be disclosed and which not. This can be accomplished by itemizing and indexing the material, and correlating indexed items with particular claims of privilege. In request of either counsel, the district court shall hold a hearing in chambers on the claim. Thereafter the court shall itself inspect the disputed items.

The president then announced that he would not comply with the order and also that he would not appeal the decision to the U.S. Supreme Court. Instead, he revealed an arrangement whereby Senator John C. Stennis of Mississippi would have access to the tapes to verify an edited summary which would be presented to the grand jury. This arrangement was accepted by the senior members of the Watergate Committee, but rejected by special prosecutor

Cox. Cox was thereupon relieved of his duties. But with no appeal forthcoming, the order to present the tapes to the District Court was in effect. The plan with Stennis was abandoned and the president's counsel announced on October 23, 1973, that the tapes would be provided under the terms and conditions set forth by the Court of Appeals.[9]

This chronology of 1973 events is pertinent to the continuing uncertainties about the scope of the executive privilege. The Court of Appeals denied an absolute privilege as determined solely by a president. But it also indicated that some protection should be accorded to information and documents or even conversations if they involved "national defense" or "state secrets." The difficulty facing the court in the search for a middle ground was how to fashion a ruling which prevented disclosure and yet permitted inspection. Even with the arrangement giving the president discretion in what was to be presented and what was to be withheld, room was left for the district judge to determine finally what was actually privileged. The burden was upon the president to present indexed material in such a manner that would convince the judge of the necessity of information control by the president. But if the judge was not convinced, the disputed information presumably would have to be supplied. If the president refused, then more fuel would be added to impeachment fires. Apparently no precedent exists on ways to force presidential compliance with a court order.

9. *CQ*, 1973, p. 2837.

VIII
Future Directions

There is no specific constitutional provision granting the president the power to refuse to give information or to deny testimony. Although a U.S. Circuit Court of Appeals in 1973 denied any absolute privilege, it was careful to indicate that the nature of the Watergate allegations warranted a limited intrusion into executive privacy and subordinated presidential claims of privilege.

The Constitution provides for three branches designed by the framers to be on a parity, one with another. In arranging for the conduct of government among the branches, degrees of independence, one from another, are given, but provision is made for cooperative action through the assignment of shared powers. It must be concluded that the intent was to ensure that no one branch could completely dominate another branch.

Within this framework government would function, but policy decisions might not always emerge quickly or smoothly or with easy agreement. This was intended and resulted in a scheme for government which has rarely been recognized or acclaimed as efficient. The history of government in the United States is saturated with evidences of conflict among the branches. If there were no conflict there would be a single dominant element, not three separate ones, and the one presumably would be the Congress. Conflict has not been destructive of the political process, and the characteristic of separateness has been recognized as a great strength for democracy, not a fundamental weakness.

It remains a curiosity, however, that the framers did not provide for equal language in setting out the powers for each of the three branches. In drafting the provisions for the Executive Article the framers were not altogether certain what the executive authority should be or what was the *executive power*. Certainly there was no reason to believe that the provisions for the Supreme Court then intended power of judicial review of executive and legislative actions as later developed. The framers gave details about the powers of the Congress because they not only were more familiar with the legislative process, but also were dealing with the very vexing problem of a federal system. Splitting the authority between the existing units, the states, and a new national authority was the more important task.

By cutting and shaping political power, therefore, the framers gave a unique character to the U.S. constitutional system. The most striking feature is the degree of independence provided for each branch.

For any of the branches, freedom from unrestricted external inquiry is essential. The Congress, primarily in subcommittee or committee deliberations, insists on some secrecy through executive or closed sessions. The judicial branch has provided for degrees of confidence and secrecy in its operations and decision-making, including some of the conduct of trials.

There is usually little objection to the controls over information and testimony exercised by the judicial branch and infrequently when exercised by the legislative branch. When the courts request information or testimony from the executive branch it may ordinarily be forthcoming and without much public notice or oratory. Most of these situations, however, involve subordinate claims of privilege, if it is invoked, and when the request is complied with there is open testimoy or *in camera* inspection or discourse in the privacy of "chambers."

When a subordinate in the executive branch claims executive privilege "as directed by the president" or the president formally invokes it in the case of congressional requests, the end result may be that some understanding or accommodation is reached, or respect is granted to the presidential decision, grudgingly given or not. Judicial demands for compliance have yet to be fully tested.

During the 1973 conflict over executive privilege in the Watergate inquiry charges were made that the president had extended it too far and exceeded any legitimate purposes in the conduct of his office. Should the privilege be invoked by the president to protect a presidential aide from testifying solely because the individual is serving as an aide, if the testimony requested would not mean any inquiry into conversations with the president or memoranda exchanged with him? Should the privilege be extended so that conversations or memoranda with third persons would be protected? To what extent may a president direct investigations concerning internal governmental matters or even matters external to them and control the uses of the results?

Although the president's statement on the executive privilege of March 12, 1973, stated that he would refuse to honor requests directed to his assistants, including those members of his cabinet who served also in an assistant assignment, and also former assistants, he modified this stand twice shortly thereafter. These modifications meant that assistants could testify about the matters under investigation in the Watergate affair. He said on May 22, 1973, that "executive privilege will not be invoked as to any testimony concerning possible criminal conduct in the matters presently under investigation, including the Watergate affair and the alleged cover-up." He did not, however, refer to conversations between himself and his assistants and presumably they remained protected in his view.[1]

During the 1971 hearing on the executive privilege, the general counsel of the American Civil Liberties Union said that "the only proper subject of executive privilege is the protection of records incidental to the making of policy, including interdepartmental memoranda, advisory opinions, recommendations of subordinates, and working papers."[2] This is a broad indication of support for the privilege, except that it does not specifically include appearances of individuals summoned. If the privilege is supportable, it would have to include appearances even if they resulted in refusals to testify at all.

Although there has been frequent and often spirited opposition to the executive privilege by members of the Congress, some of these critics have indicated not only its desirability, but also its necessity, *if* restricted to certain situations and conditions. These situations and conditions reflect some of the uses of the privilege which have prevailed throughout its history. During the 1971 hearings, Senator Ervin, one of the most forceful opponents of the privilege, endorsed its exercise if it involved some national security matters, such as to protect information which might imperil the safety of military forces, and the disclosure of contemplated military movements, and transportation of troops. "Information of that sort," he stated,

1. A president may want to have unquestioned loyalty from his immediate staff, but it is unlikely that he could command blind obedience. Violations of nondisclosure directives could be subject to punishment if they involved classified material. Former assistants to the president who would ignore a directive such as the March, 1973, statement by President Nixon would suffer no direct penalties except subsequent presidential disfavor. Those on his staff who would violate the directive would probably suffer nothing beyond dismissal. It should be noted, however, that in *Gravel* v. *U.S.*, decided on June 29, 1972, Justice White, for the majority of the U.S. Supreme Court, said that the "so-called executive privilege has never been applied to shield executive officers from prosecution for crime."

2. Senate, *Hearing*, 1971, p. 368.

"would be certainly something the Executive would have the power to withhold."[3] Other uses which he pinpointed included information necessary to enable the government to prepare a case for trial in the courts, and some working papers of the executive branch, but not all of them. The 1971 refusal to provide projections for foreign military assitance, for example, would have minimal congressional support.

Congressional endorsement of the privilege would be unlikely for general claims of immunity and certainly not by subordinates. The advice privilege has many supporters, especially when it involves discussions or opinions or memoranda exchanged with the president personally. Respect for the presidency would probably dominate in any congressional effort avowing unlimited authority to set forth all conditions under which the executive privilege could be invoked.

The executive privilege should be invoked only personally by a president. It should be called the Executive privilege—with a capital *E*—and not be used as a recourse to privilege generally.

This examination of the uses of the privilege and the issues resulting from its exercise shows that it has been successfully invoked on many occasions, even with some resulting accommodation in the contests for executive branch information or testimony. In several instances, of course, presidents have revised their positions and have granted requests in whole or in part.

When a president is confronted with a threat to subpoena his records, or as in the case of Jefferson at the time of the Burr trial or Nixon in the Watergate controversy, when subpoenas were actually issued, several options are available. Jefferson refused to comply with a request for a personal appearance but later provided the wanted information. Nixon initially refused to comply with

3. Ibid., pp. 251, 252.

a request for the recorded information ordered by the U.S. District Court and hoped for a successful decision by the appellate court on appeal. The latter failing, he chose nation-wide addresses, news conferences, visits with members of the Congress and with some governors. Concurrently, however, he arranged that the subpoenaed tapes be reviewed *in camera* by the U.S. judge, who would determine which conversations were pertinent to the inquiry.[4]

The decision of the Court of Appeals on October 12, 1973, included these words: "It is the courts that determine the validity of the assertion and scope of the privilege." That decision denied any absolute executive privilege to be determined solely by a president. "If the claim of absolute privilege was recognized, its mere invocation by the President or his surrogate could deny access to all documents in all the executive departments of all citizens and their representatives, including Congress, the courts as well as grand juries, state governments, state officials and all state subdivisions." But the court did not deny that documents and conversations are often so intertwined that they may be rendered inseparable. Thus, the president could decline to transmit such portions and ask the district court to reconsider whether *in camera* inspection was necessary. If the court agreed, then no disclosure even *in camera* would occur. Unquestionably Nixon's actions to agree were guided by ethical and political considerations more persuasive then the subpoena.

4. George Washington, in 1795, in an issue with Secretary of State Edmund Randolph, authorized Randolph to "publish, without reserve, any and every private and confidential letter I ever wrote you: nay more: every word I have ever uttered in your presence." Presumably this was to help vindicate Randolph, who had been accused of deception in a policy shift in the final provisions of the Jay Treaty, but Washington also had another motive. Release of the information by Randolph would be far less damaging than the implication that Washington had matters to hide that might be assumed to involve him personally. Randolph later wrote Washington that he would not exhibit to public view "*all* and *everything* which was known to me." The letters are included in Edmund Randolph, *A Vindication of Mr. Randolph's Resignation* (Philadelphia: Samuel H. Smith, 1795), pp. 25–26.

The appellate court recognized the dangers of disclosing sensitive national security matters and of wholesale public access to executive deliberations. If allowed, these would cripple the "executive as a co-equal branch." The court also concluded that its order to the president "represents an unusual and limited requirement that the President produce material evidence. . . . The Constitution mentions no executive privilege, much less any absolute executive privilege." In the court's view, determination of the extent of presidential control over information would have to be shared with the judicial branch, but it also recognized the need for a president to control confidences and appeared to base its course on the uniqueness of the proceedings where wrongdoing was alleged and where information held by the president would be final proof about it. This decision should not be construed, however, as a scrapping of the executive privilege. "We end, as we began, by emphasizing the extraordinary nature of this case. We have attempted no more then the problem before us—a problem that takes its unique shape from the grand jury's compelling showing of need." It was a need in the judicial process and an inquiry into possible criminal acts which were at the root of the issue, not a test of a desire by the legislative branch for the information.

If the privilege were determined to be subject to congressional definition, it would not mean, necessarily, that the Congress would extend no protection at all. There would be recognition that in the conduct of executive affairs some confidences are necessary. This recognition is given in the Freedom of Information Act as was tested successfully, in part, in *Environmental Protection Agency* v. *Mink.*[5]

5. Op. cit. When Sherman Adams, assistant to President Eisenhower, declined to accept a formal invitation to appear before a Senate subcommittee investigating the Dixon-Yates contract, he relied on his "official and confidential relationship with the President." See U.S. Congress, Senate, *Power Policy: Dixon Yates Contract, Hearings on S. Res. 61 before the Subcommittee on Antitrust and Monopoly of the Senate Committee on the Judiciary*, 84th Cong., 1st sess., 1955, p. 676.

If charges of personal wrongdoing for "treason, bribery, or other high crimes and misdemeanors" were made against a president, the impeachment route would be the appropriate one, but it would not necessarily break any presidential silence. Suggestions of wrongdoing because of his knowledge of criminal acts by others, especially by his own staff, could pose possible difficult distinctions whether he had been guilty of "high crimes and misdemeanors."

The executive privilege may defy successful definition. By its very nature the executive power does not lend itself to any easy setting out of the limits of that power. Furthermore, efforts to compel disclosure suggest that a president should be a witness against himself, and disclosures from subordinates could have that result. Any president should be unwilling to submit himself to such an ordeal and presumably would use all his influence to prevent it.

The Congress has been able to obtain needed information to fulfill its responsibilities and has not been unduly hampered because of the exercise of the executive privilege.[6] On those occasions when a clash has resulted between the president and the Congress the issue at the moment has often been exaggerated out of proportion. The conflict may well be deeply enmeshed in the practical workings of the political affairs of government and society. The issue may be a real and significant one, but the restraints imposed on information or testimony by a president may be for reasons more compelling than any need to know. When the compelling public interest is the dominant one and the need to know superior to a claim of privilege, the outcome likely will follow the pattern of other issues: a pragmatic approach will be arrived at ultimately

6. There is no question that requested information or testimony from the executive departments and agencies has been provided slowly or reluctantly or not at all, at least not to the satisfaction of many of the members of the Congress.

wherein compromises are reached. This has been the history of the uses of the executive privilege. Modifications of positions are made and demands for publicly given testimony are softened to permit some testimony in private and refusals for information are altered to provide for a part of that which was requested.

Neither the Congress nor the president is ever quite certain of their "rights" involving executive privilege. It is in the nature of constitutional government in the United States that the legislative, executive, and judicial powers are always in some transitory stage. This has been the development of the tripartite system from the beginning and there is little evidence that finite relationships or arrangements can or should be provided to set them out for all future time.

Appendix

I. *In January 1807, the following resolution was passed by the House of Representatives and addressed to Thomas Jefferson. The information requested related to the military expedition headed by Aaron Burr.*

Resolved, That the President of the United States be, and he hereby is, requested to lay before this House any information in possession of the Executive, *except such as he may deem the public welfare to require not to be disclosed*, touching any illegal combination of private individuals against the peace and safety of the Union, or any military expedition planned by such individuals against the territories of any Power in amity with the United States; together with the measures which the Executive has pursued and proposed to take for suppressing or defeating the same. [*Emphasis supplied.*]

II. *The following letter was President Franklin D. Roosevelt's reply to the request by the House of Representatives of May 6, 1935, for a full text of the President's press conference of May 3, 1935, on resolutions of the U.S. Chamber of Commerce about his legislative program. The resolution stated, however, that the text should be provided "if agreeable to him."*

My Dear Mr. Speaker:

I wish very much that you would thank the House of Representatives, and Congressman John Martin of Colorado in particular, for the opportunity given me in

House Resolution 212 to transmit the transcript of my conference with the press wherein I spoke of the historic attitude of certain types of business organizations toward legislative proposals which have been introduced in the Congress of the United States and in many State legislatures the last 20 years or more. I do appreciate this opportunity.

I do not believe, however, that it would be advisable for me to create the precedent of sending to the Congress for documentary use the text of remarks I make at the bi-weekly conference with the newspaper representatives here in Washington.

It is my desire that these conferences should be continued on the free and open basis which I have endeavored to maintain at all times. To create the precedent of permitting questions and answers which come up at a press conference to be transcribed and printed in the Congressional Record or other official documents would mean that I no longer would feel like speaking extemporaneously and informally, as is my habit, and it would bring me a consciousness of restraint as well as a necessity for constant preparation of my remarks. The simple truth is that I do not have the time to give to such preparation for a press conference.

I much prefer to continue the conferences in the free and informal fashion. The newspaper men, except where particular permission is given, do not directly quote the statements I make to them. They do, however, use them in substance, and the press reports generally published following the conference of Friday, May 3 last, present an accurate record of the statements I made at that time. As a matter of fact, there would be little difference between the transcript of this conference and the published reports except that one would be in the nature of direct quotation and the other would be indirect.

Very sincerely yours,
Franklin D. Roosevelt

III. *At the time of an inquiry into operations of the Federal Communications Commission in 1944, Attorney General Francis Biddle wrote the chairman of the select committee of the House of Representatives outlining reasons why J. Edgar Hoover, director of the Federal Bureau of Investigation, should not respond to some of the questions put to him by the committee. The letter is dated January 24, 1944.*

My Dear Mr. Chairman:

I have carefully considered the request of Mr. Garey, counsel for the committee, that I produce before your committee a copy of the document that I received from the President directing Mr. Hoover not to testify before your committee about certain transactions between this department and the Federal Communications Commission.

It is my view that as a matter of law and of long-established constitutional practice, communications between the President and the Attorney General are confidential and privileged and not subject to inquiry by a committee of one of the Houses of Congress. In this instance, it seems to me that the privilege should not be waived; to do so would be to establish an unfortunate precedent, inconsistent with the position taken by my predecessors.

It could, moreover, open the door to detailed inquiries into the confidential and privileged relationship that exists between the President and the Attorney General, heretofore generally recognized by the Congress. I must therefore respectfully decline to produce before your committee the President's communication. Without waiving in any way the privilege, however, I believe that I can inform the committee that the President's directive states that because the transactions relate to the internal security of the country, it would not be in the public interest, at the present time, for Mr. Hoover or any officer of the Department to testify about them or to disclose any correspondence concerning them.

Furthermore, I should like to point out that a number

of Mr. Garey's questions related to the methods and results of investigations carried on by the Federal Bureau of Investigation. The Department of Justice has consistently taken the position, long acquiesced in by the Congress, that it is not in the public interest to have these matters publicly disclosed. Even in the absence of instructions from the President, therefore, I should have directed Mr. Hoover to refuse to answer these questions.

I note from the transcript of the hearing held by your committee on January 20, 1944, that Mr. Hoover has been requested to return on the morning of Tuesday, January 25. I also note that Mr. Garey has stated that the general subjects as to which he wishes to examine Mr. Hoover were all touched upon in one form or another during the course of his examination on January 20, 1944. The transcript of that examination shows that these subjects fall within the scope of the direction given by the President. If Mr. Hoover appears again before the committee, he would be obliged again to decline to testify as to these matters. I hope you will agree with me that no useful purpose will be served by a repetition of Mr. Hoover's refusal to testify. Certainly, no additional hearing is required to indicate the scope of Mr. Garey's questions or Mr. Hoover's refusals to answer. In view of the heavy demands made upon Mr. Hoover's time by his official responsibilities, I respectfully suggest that he should be excused from further attendance before the committee.

Sincerely yours,
Francis Biddle, Attorney General

IV. *Upon receiving a subpoena issued by the chairman of the House Un-American Activities Committee in November, 1953, President Harry S Truman wrote a reply refusing to comply and gave his reasons. The letter is reproduced below.*

Dear Sir:

I have your subpoena dated Nov. 9, 1953, directing my appearance before your committee on Friday, Nov.

13, in Washington. The subpoena does not state the matters upon which you seek my testimony, but I assume from the press stories that you seek to examine me with respect to matters which occurred during my tenure of the Presidency of the United States.

In spite of my personal willingness to cooperate with your committee, I feel constrained by my duty to the people of the United States to decline to comply with the subpoena.

In doing so, I am carrying out the provisions of the Constitution of the United States; and am following a long line of precedents, commencing with George Washington himself in 1796. Since his day, Presidents Jefferson, Monroe, Jackson, Tyler, Polk, Fillmore, Buchanan, Lincoln, Grant, Hayes, Cleveland, Theodore Roosevelt, Coolidge, Hoover and Franklin D. Roosevelt have declined to respond to subpoenas or demands for information of various kinds by Congress.

The underlying reason for this clearly established and universally recognized constitutional doctrine has been succinctly set forth by Charles Warren, one of our leading constitutional authorities, as follows:

> In this long series of contests by the Executive to maintain his constitutional integrity, one sees a legitimate conclusion from our theory of government. . . . Under our Constitution, each branch of the Government is designed to be a coordinate representative of the will of the people. . . . Defense by the Executive of his constitutional powers becomes in very truth, therefore, defense of popular rights—defense of power which the people granted to him.
>
> It was in that sense that President Cleveland spoke of his duty to the people not to relinquish any of the powers of his great office. It was in that sense that President Buchanan stated the people have rights and prerogatives in the execution of his office by the President which every President is under a duty to see "shall never be violated in his person" but "passed to his successors unimpaired by the adoption of a dangerous precedent." In maintaining his

> rights against a trespassing Congress, the President defends not himself, but popular government; he represents not himself but the people.

President Jackson repelled an attempt by the Congress to break down the separation of powers in these words:

> For myself I shall repell all such attempts as an invasion of the principles of justice as well as of the Constitution, and I shall esteem it my sacred duty to the people of the United States to resist them as I would the establishment of a Spanish Inquisition.

I might commend to your reading the opinion of one of the committees of the House of Representatives in 1879, House Report 141, March 3, 1879, Forty-fifth Congress, Third Session, in which the House Judiciary Committee said the following:

> The Executive is as independent of either house of Congress as either house of Congress is independent of him, and they cannot call for the records of his actions, or the action of his officers against his consent, any more than he can call for any of the journals or records of the House or Senate.

It must be obvious to you that if the doctrine of separation of powers and the independence of the Presidency is to have any validity at all, it must be equally applicable to a President after his term of office has expired when he is sought to be examined with respect to any acts occurring while he is President.

The doctrine would be shattered, and the President, contrary to our fundamental theory of constitutional government, would become a mere arm of the Legislative Branch of the Government if he would feel during his term of office that his every act might be subject to official inquiry and possible distortion for political purposes.

If your intention, however, is to inquire into any acts as a private individual either before or after my Presidency and unrelated to any acts as President, I shall be happy to appear.

Yours very truly,
Harry S. Truman

V. *The following letters, one from Representative John E. Moss and the other from President Kennedy, are representative of similar exchanges between Moss and Presidents Johnson and Nixon. They show the distinctions these presidents made about privileged information and the invoking of the executive privilege by a president.*

Special Government Information Subcommittee,
of the Committee on Government Operations,
Washington, D.C., February 15, 1962.

Hon. John F. Kennedy,
President of the United States,
The White House,
Washington, D.C.

Dear Mr. President:

In your letter of February 8, 1962 to Secretary McNamara you directed him to refuse certain information to a Senate Subcommittee. The concluding paragraph of your letter stated:

> "The principle which is at stake here cannot be automatically applied to every request for information. Each case must be judged on its merits."

A similar letter from President Eisenhower on May 17, 1954 also refused information to a Senate Subcommittee, setting forth the same arguments covered in your letter. President Eisenhower did not, however, state that future questions of availability of information to the Congress would have to be answered as they came up.

I know you are aware of the result of President Eisenhower's letter. Time after time Executive Branch employees far down the administrative line from the President fell back on his letter of May 17, 1954 as authority to withhold information from the Congress and the public.

Some of the cases are well known—the Dixon-Yates matter and the investigation of East-West trade controls, for instance—but many of the refusals based on President Eisenhower's letter of May 17, 1954 received no public notice. A report of the House Committee on Government Operations covering the five years from June, 1955 through June, 1960 lists 44 cases of Executive Branch officials refusing information on the basis of the principles set forth in the May 17, 1954 letter.

I am confident that you share by belief that your letter of February 8, 1962 to Secretary McNamara should not be seized upon by Executive Branch employees—many of them holding the same policy-making positions of responsibility they did under the Eisenhower Administration—as a new claim of authority to withhold information from the Congress and the public. A Subcommittee staff study indicates that during the year between the time you took office and February 8, 1962, the claim of an "executive privilege" to withhold government information was not used successfully once, compared to the dozens of times in previous years administrative employees held up "executive privilege" as a shield against public and Congressional access to information.

Although your letter of February 8, 1962 stated clearly that the principle involved could not be applied automatically to restrict information, this warning received little public notice. Clarification of this point would, I believe, serve to prevent the rash of restrictions on government information which followed the May 17, 1954 letter from President Eisenhower.

Sincerely,
(s) John E. Moss, Chairman

The White House
Washington, March 7, 1962.

Hon. John E. Moss,
Chairman, Special Government Information Subcommittee of the Committee on Government Operations

Dear Mr. Chairman:

This is in reply to your letter of last month inquiring generally about the practice this Administration will follow in invoking the doctrine of executive privilege in withholding certain information from the Congress.

As your letter indicated, my letter of February 8 to Secretary McNamara made it perfectly clear that the directive to refuse to make certain specific information available to a special subcommittee of the Senate Armed Services Committee was limited to that specific request and that "each case must be judged on its merits."

As you know, this Administration has gone to great lengths to achieve full cooperation with the Congress in making available to it all appropriate documents, correspondence and information. That is the basic policy of this Administration, and it will continue to be so. Executive privilege can be invoked only by the President and will not be used without specific Presidential approval. Your own interest in assuring the widest public accessibility to governmental information is, of course, well known, and I can assure you this Administration will continue to cooperate with your subcommittee and the entire Congress in achieving this objective.

Sincerely,
(s) John F. Kennedy.

VI. *On March 5, 1971, Senator J. William Fulbright and Senator Alan Cranston introduced S. 1125, designed to limit the exercise of the executive privilege. Later, on July 29, 1971, Fulbright presented a series of amendments to the proposal. The language of the original bill is given first, followed by the amendments.*

. . . Executive Privilege

(a) An Employee of the executive branch summoned or requested to testify or produce documents before Congress, any joint committee of the Congress, any committee of either House of the Congress, or any subcommittee of any such committee, who intends to exercise executive privilege as to the whole or any portion of the matter about which he was summoned, requested to testify, or produce documents, shall not refuse to appear on the gounds that he intends to assert executive privilege.

(b) In no case shall an employee of the executive branch appearing before the Congress, any joint committee of the Congress, any committee of either House of the Congress, or any subcommittee of any such committee, in response to a summons or request, assert executive privilege unless the employee presents, at the time executive privilege is asserted in response to any testimony or document sought, a statement signed personally by the President requiring that the employees assert executive privilege as to the testimony or document sought.

Amendments

. . . Availability of information to Congress and the General Accounting Office

(a) The Congress declares that information of, or under the custody or control of, any agency of the Government is to be made available to the Congress so that the Congress may exercise, in an informed manner, the authority conferred upon it by article I of the Constitution to make laws necessary and proper to carry into execution the powers vested in the Congress and all other powers vested in that Government or any department or officer thereof.

(b) For the purpose of this section—

(1) "agency" means—

(A) an executive agency;

(B) a military department; and

(C) the government of the District of Columbia;

(2) "employee" means—

(A) an employee in or under an agency; and

(B) a member of the uniformed services;

(3) "Government" means the Government of the United States and the government of the District of Columbia; and

(4) "information" includes any information, paper, record, report, or document.

(c) Any information of, or under the custody or control of, any agency or employee of that agency shall be made available to any joint committee of the Congress, any committee of either House of the Congress, any subcommittee of any such committee, or the General Accounting Office, upon request of any such committee, subcommittee, or office for information relating to matters within the jurisdiction of the committee, subcommittee, or office making the request, unless executive privilege is invoked with respect to that information and is invoked in accordance with this section.

(d) Executive privilege shall be invoked with respect to any information so requested only if the President signs a statement invoking such privilege with respect to that information requested.

(e) (1) Any information requested by any such committee, subcommittee, or office shall be furnished immediately unless the head of the agency which receives the request determines, as soon as practicable after receiving the request, that the information requested is information with respect to which the head of the agency believes there are compelling circumstances for invoking executive privilege. If the head of the agency so determines, he shall immediately inform the committee, subcommittee, or office requesting the information of his belief and shall consult with the Attorney General or his designee to obtain advice on the question whether to seek invocation of the privilege by the President.

(2) If, after a prompt and thorough consideration, the head of the agency and the Attorney General or his designee agree that compelling circumstances do not exist for invoking executive privilege, the information requested shall be made available immediately to the committee, subcommittee, or office requesting that information. If the head of the agency and the Attorney General

or his designee believe that compelling circumstances exist for invoking executive privilege, they shall recommend to the President in writing that the privilege be invoked. If thirty days after an agency has received a request for information, no such recommendation has been transmitted to the President, such information shall be made available immediately to the committee, subcommittee, or office requesting the information.

(3) If the President invokes executive privilege with respect to any information requested, such committee, subcommittee, or office requesting the information shall be furnished promptly with a statement by the President in writing giving his reasons for invoking executive privilege with respect to the information so requested. If the President does not invoke executive privilege with respect to information so requested within thirty days after a recommendation seeking invocation of the privilege has been transmitted to the President, such information shall be made available immediately to the committee, subcommittee, or office requesting that information.

(f) If the General Accounting Office determines that any information requested of an agency by any such committee, subcommittee, or office has not been made available within a period of sixty days after the request has been received by that agency, and if during such period the President has not signed a statement invoking executive privilege with respect to that information, no funds made available to that agency shall be obligated or expended commencing on the seventieth day after such request is received by such agency or employee of that agency, unless and until such information is made available or the President invokes executive privilege with respect to such information.

VII. *The following letter was sent to the chairman of the Senate Committee on the Judiciary on April 10, 1972, by John W. Dean III, counsel to the president, in response to an invitation from the committee that Peter M. Flanigan, assistant to the president, testify before the committee concerning the ITT antitrust settlement.*

Dear Mr. Chairman:

On Friday afternoon, April 7, 1972, Mr. John Holloman of your staff telephoned Mr. Peter Flanigan, Assistant to the President, to invite him to appear and testify before your Committee on April 12, 1972, at 10:30 AM, in connection with the Committee's hearings relating to the confirmation of Mr. Richard G. Kleindienst as Attorney General. This letter is in response to the Committee's invitation.

Mr. Flanigan is one of the Assistants to the President provided for in Sections 105 and 106 of Title 3 of the United States Code. Under the doctrine of separation of powers, and long established historical precedents, the principle that members of the President's immediate staff not appear and testify before congressional committees with respect to the performance of their duties is firmly established. Accordingly, by reason of this long established and fundamental principle of our federal system, Mr. Flanigan cannot accept the Committee's invitation to appear on April 12, 1972.

Mr. Flanigan's name has been brought into the discussion during the present hearings in connection with the efforts of former Assistant Attorney General McLaren to obtain independent financial expertise to assist in evaluating financial aspects of the ITT antitrust suits. After reviewing the transcripts of your hearings to date with Mr. Flanigan, I can and do certify to you and your Committee that Mr. Flanigan's involvement in this matter was stated by Judge McLaren in his sworn testimony. Mr. Flanigan merely responded to Mr. McLaren's request to assist him in obtaining such expertise. I might also add that Mr. Flanigan did not directly or indirectly contribute to the findings or conclusions of the independent expert.

Respectfully yours,
John W. Dean III,
Counsel to the President.

VIII. *During the controversy between the president and the Senate in 1972 over whether executive agreements with Portugal and Bahrain should be submitted to the Senate as treaties, the following measure was proposed for enactment by the Congress:*

Be it enacted by the Senate and House of Representatives of the United States of America in Congress assembled, That (a) the Congress declares that, until the Agreements signed by the United States with Portugal and Bahrain, relating to the use by the United States of military bases in the Azores and Bahrain have been submitted to the Senate as treaties for its advice and consent, assistance to be furnished Portugal and Bahrain as the result of such Agreements should be terminated, and that Senate Resolution 214, 92nd Congress, agreed to March 3, 1972, expressed the sense of the Senate that such Agreements should be so submitted to the Senate as treaties.

(b) Therefore, notwithstanding any other provisions of law, of and after the date of enactment of this Act—

(1) No vessel shall be loaned or otherwise made available to Portugal;

(2) No agricultural commodities may be sold to Portugal for dollars on credit terms or for foreign currencies under the Agricultural Trade and Assistance Act of 1954;

(3) No funds may be provided to Portugal for educational projects out of amounts made available to the Department of Defense;

(4) No excess articles may be provided by any means to Portugal;

(5) No defense articles may be ordered for Portugal from the stocks of the Department of Defense under section 506 of the Foreign Assistance Act of 1961; and

(6) The Export-Import Bank of the United States may not guarantee, insure, extend credit, or participate in any extension of credit, with respect to the purchase or lease of any product by Portugal, or any agency or

national thereof, or with respect to the purchase or lease of any product by another foreign country or agency or national thereof if the Bank has knowledge that the product is to be purchased or leased to Portugal until such agreement with Portugal is submitted to the Senate as a treaty for its advice and consent.

(c) Notwithstanding any other provisions of law, on and after the date of enactment of this Act, no funds may be furnished by the United States to Bahrain for the use of any such base on Bahrain until such Agreement is submitted to the Senate as a treaty for its advice and consent.

[*The proposal was not enacted.*]

IX. *The following is the White House text of President Richard M. Nixon's March 12, 1973, policy statement on the executive privilege.*

During my press conference of January 31, 1973, I stated that I would issue a statement outlining my views on executive privilege.

The doctrine of executive privilege is well established. It was first invoked by President Washington, and it has been recognized and utilized by our Presidents for almost 200 years since that time. The doctrine is rooted in the Constitution, which vests "the Executive Power" solely in the President, and it is designed to protect communications within the executive branch in a variety of circumstances in time of both war and peace.

Without such protection, our military security, our relations with other countries, our law enforcement procedures and many other aspects of the national interest could be significantly damaged and the decision-making process of the executive branch could be impaired.

General Policy

The general policy of this Administration regarding the use of executive privilege during the next four years will be the same as the one we have followed during the past four years and which I outlined in my press conference: executive privilege will not be used as a shield to prevent embarrassing information from being made available but will be exercised only in those particular instances in which disclosure would harm the public interest.

I first enunciated this policy in a memorandum of March 24, 1969, which I sent to Cabinet officers and heads of agencies. The memorandum read in part:

> The policy of this Administration is to comply to the fullest extent possible with Congressional requests for information. While the Executive branch has the responsibility of withholding certain information the disclosure of which would be incompatible with the public interest, this Administration will invoke this authority only in the most compelling circumstances and after a rigorous inquiry into the actual need for its exercise. For those reasons Executive privilege will not be used without specific Presidential approval.

In recent weeks, questions have been raised about the availability of officials in the executive branch to present testimony before committees of the Congress. As my 1969 memorandum dealt primarily with guidelines for providing information to the Congress and did not focus specifically on appearances by officers of the executive branch and members of the President's personal staff, it would be useful to outline my policies concerning the latter question.

Three Invocations

During the first four years of my Presidency, hundreds of Administration officials spent thousands of hours freely testifying before Committees of the Congress. Secretary of Defense Laird, for instance, made 86 separate appearances before Congressional committees, engaging in over 327 hours of testimony. By contrast, there were only three occasions during the first term of my Administration when executive privilege was invoked anywhere in the executive branch in response to a Congressional request for information. These facts speak not of a closed administration, but of one that is pledged to openness and is proud to stand on its record.

Requests for Congressional appearances by members of the President's personal staff present a different situation and raise different considerations. Such requests have been relatively infrequent through the years, and in past administrations they have been routinely declined. I have followed that same tradition in my Administration, and I intend to continue it during the remainder of my term.

Under the doctrine of separation of powers, the manner in which the President personally exercises his assigned executive powers is not subject to questioning by another branch of Government. If the President is not subject to such questioning, it is equally appropriate that members of his staff not be so questioned, for their roles are in effect an extension of the Presidency.

Executive Integrity

This tradition rests on more than Constitutional doctrine: it is also a practical necessity. To insure the effective discharge of the executive responsibility, a President must be able to place absolute confidence in the advice and assistance offered by the members of his staff. And in the performance of their duties for the President, those staff members must not be inhibited by the possibility that their advice and assistance will ever become a matter of public debate, either during their tenure in Government or at a later date. Otherwise, the candor with which advice is rendered and the quality of such assistance will inevitably be compromised and weakened. What is at stake, therefore, is not simply a question of confidentiality but the integrity of the decision-making process at the very highest levels of our Government.

The considerations I have just outlined have been and

must be recognized in other fields, in and out of government. A law clerk, for instance, is not subject to interrogation about the factors or discussions that preceded a decision of the judge.

For these reasons, just as I shall not invoke executive privilege lightly, I shall also look to the Congress to continue this proper tradition in asking for executive branch testimony only from the officers properly constituted to provide the information sought, and only when the eliciting of such testimony will serve a genuine legislative purpose.

As I stated in my press conference on January 31, the question of whether circumstances warrant the exercise of executive privilege should be determined on a case-by-case basis. In making such decisions, I shall rely on the following guidelines:

Guidelines

(1) In the case of a department or agency, every official shall comply with a reasonable request for an appearance before the Congress, provided that the performance of the duties of his office will not be seriously impaired thereby. If the official believes that a Congressional request for a particular document or for testimony on a particular point raises a substantial question as to the need for invoking executive privilege, he shall comply with the procedures set forth in my memorandum of March 24, 1969. Thus, executive privilege will not be invoked until the compelling need for its exercise has been clearly demonstrated and the request has been approved first by the Attorney General and then by the President.

(2) A Cabinet officer or any other Government official who also holds a position as a member of the President's personal staff shall comply with any reasonable request to testify in his non-White House capacity, provided that the performance of his duties will not be seriously impaired

thereby. If the official believes that the request raises a substantial question as to the need for invoking executive privilege, he shall comply with the procedures set forth in my memorandum of March 24, 1969.

(3) A member or former member of the President's personal staff normally shall follow the well-established precedent and decline a request for a formal appearance before a committee of the Congress. At the same time, it will continue to be my policy to provide all necessary and relevant information through informal contact between my present staff and committees of the Congress in ways which preserve intact the Constitutional separation of the branches.

X. *On February 28, 1973, seven members of the House of Representatives introduced H.R. 4938, which was designed to extend controls over the executive privilege. It is presented in full.*

A BILL

To amend the Freedom of Information Act to require that all information be made available to Congress except where Executive privilege is invoked.

Be it enacted by the Senate and House of Representatives of the United States of America in Congress assembled, That section 552 of title 5 of the United States Code (the Freedom of Information Act) is amended by adding at the end thereof the following:

(d) (1) Whenever either House of Congress, any committee thereof (to the extent of matter within its jurisdiction), or the Comptroller General of the United States, requests an agency to make available information within its possession or under its control, the head of such agency shall make the information available as soon as practicable but not later than thirty days from the date of the request unless in the interim a statement is submitted by the President or by an agency head signed by the President invoking

Executive privilege as the basis upon which the information is being refused.

(2) Whenever either House of Congress or any committee thereof (to the extent of matter within its jurisdiction) requests the presence of an officer or employee of an agency for testimony regarding matters within the agency's possession or under its control, the officer or employee shall appear and supply all information requested except that such officer or employee may refuse to supply those items of information specifically ordered withheld by the President in a signed statement in which Executive privilege is invoked.

(3) Executive privilege shall be invoked only by the President and only in those instances in which the requested information or testimony contains policy recommendations made to the President or agency head and the President determines that disclosure of such information will seriously jeopardize the national interest and his ability or that of the agency head to obtain forthright advice. To the extent possible, however, factual information underlying policy recommendations shall be made available in response to a request.

(4) "Agency," as used in this subsection, means department, agency, instrumentality, or other authority of Government of the United States (other than the Congress or courts of the United States), including any establishment within the Executive Office of the President.

XI. *On April 17, 1973, President Nixon modified his position announced on March 12 that presidential aides would not be permitted to testify before congressional committees. Agreement was reached between members of the Senate Select Committee on Presidential Campaign Activities and members of the president's staff on ground rules to be observed. The president's statement, however, indicates that aides would testify before the committee only where wrongdoing was charged and that the agreement would not apply to other hearings. The Nixon statement follows, in part:*

I believe now an agreement has been reached which is satisfactory to both sides. The committee ground rules as adopted totally preserve the doctrine of separation of powers. They provide that the appearance by a witness may, in the first instance, be in executive session, if appropriate.

Second, executive privilege is expressly reserved and may be asserted during the course of the questioning as to any questions.

Now, much as been made of the issue as to whether the proceedings could be televised. To me, this has never been a central issue, especially if the separation of powers problem is otherwise solved, as I now think it is.

All members of the White House staff will appear voluntarily when requested by the committee. They will testify under oath and they will answer fully all proper questions.

I should point out that this arrangement is one that covers this hearing only in which wrongdoing has been charged. This kind of arrangement, of course, would not apply to other hearings. Each of them will be considered on its merits.

XII. *On April 18, 1973, the Senate Select Committee on Presidential Campaign Activities announced guidelines it would follow in dealing with witnesses who would appear before it. The committee was popularly known as the Watergate Committee.*

1. The committee will receive oral and documentary evidence relevant to the matters S. Res. 60 authorizes it to investigate and matters bearing on the credibility of the witnesses who testify before it.

2. All witnesses shall testify before the committee on oath or affirmation in hearings which shall be open to the public and the news media. This guideline shall not abridge, however, the power of the committee to take the testimony of a particular witness on oath or affirmation in an executive meeting if the committee would otherwise

be unable to ascertain whether the witness knows anything relevant to the matters the committee is authorized to investigate.

3. All still and motion picture photography will be completed before a witness actually testifies, and no such photography shall occur while the witness is testifying. Television coverage of a witness and his testimony shall be permitted, however, under the provisions of the standing rules of the committee.

4. In taking the testimony of a witness, the committee will endeavor to do two things: First, to minimize inconvenience to the witness and disruption of his affairs; and, second, to afford the witness a fair opportunity to give testimony without undue interruption.

To achieve the first of these objectives, the committee will honor the request of the witness to the extent feasible for advance notice of the time and place appointed for taking his testimony with as much dispatch as circumstances permit, and release the witness from further attendance on the committee as soon as circumstances allow, subject, however, to the power of the committee to recall him for further testimony in the event the committee deems such action advisable.

To afford the witness a fair opportunity to present his testimony, the committee will permit the witness to make an opening statement not exceeding 20 minutes, which shall not be interrupted by questioning, and a closing statement summarizing his testimony, not exceeding five minutes, which will not be interrupted by questioning: Provided, however, questions suggested by the closing statement may be propounded after such statement is made.

5. The committee respects and recognizes the right of a prospective witness who is interviewed by the staff of the committee in advance of a public hearing as well as the right of a witness who appears before the committee

to be accompanied by a lawyer of his own choosing to advise him concerning his constitutional and legal rights as a witness.

6. If the lawyer who accompanies a witness before the committee advises the witness to claim a privilege against giving any testimony sought by the committee, the committee shall have the discretionary power to permit the lawyer to present his views on the matter for the information of the committee, and the committee shall thereupon rule on the validity of the claim or its application to the particular circumstances involved and require the witness to give testimony sought in the event its ruling on the claim is adverse to the witness.

Neither the witness nor any other officer or person shall be permitted to claim a privilege against the witness testifying prior to the appearance of the witness before the committee, and the committee shall not rule in respect to the claim until the question by which the testimony is sought is put to the witness.

7. The committee believes that it may be necessary for it to obtain the testimony of some White House aides if the committee is to be able to ascertain the complete truth in respect to the matters it is authorized to investigate by S. Res. 60.

To this end, the committee will invite such White House aides as it has reason to believe have knowledge of information relevant to the matters it is authorized to investigate to appear before the committee and give testimony on oath or affirmation respecting such matters.

In this connection, the committee will extend to such aides the considerations set forth in detail in Guideline No. 4 and the right to counsel set forth in detail in Guidelines Nos. 5 and 6.

In addition to these considerations and rights, the committee will permit the White House to have its own counsel present when any White House aide appears before the committee as a witness, and permit such counsel to invoke any claim that a privilege available to the President forbids a White House aide to give the testimony sought by the committee, and the committee shall thereupon rule on validity of such claim or its application to the particular testimony sought in the manner and with the effect set forth in Guideline No. 6 in respect to a claim of privilege invoked by a witness or his counsel.

The committee will not subpoena a White House aide to appear before it or its staff unless such aide fails to make timely response to an invitation to appear.

8. The committee may require the sergeant-at-arms of the Senate, or any of his assistants or deputies, or any available law-enforcement officer to eject from a meeting of the committee any person who willfully disrupts the meeting or willfully impedes the committee in the performance of its functions under S. Res. 60.

9. Whenever the committee takes testimony through the agency of less than the majority of the members of the committee as authorized by its standing rules, the member or members of the committee taking the testimony shall be vested with the powers set forth in these guidelines and shall be deemed to act as the committee in exercising such powers.

Index